Both Sides Now

Both Sides Now

Published by the
Northern Ireland Mixed Marriage Association
28 Bedford Street, Belfast BT2 7FE

Printed by
Nova Print & Design
Twin Spires, Northumberland St, Belfast BT13 2JF
ISBN 978-0-9571669-2-9
© 2015

Foreword

The Northern Ireland 'Troubles' had already claimed their 1,000th victim when a group of young couples came together in 1974 to form the Northern Ireland Mixed Marriage Association (NIMMA). More than 40 years later, those dark days seem like light years away.

NIMMA's hardworking volunteers have helped increase public awareness of mixed marriage, foster tolerance and, today, they continue to address individual pastoral needs, as well as lobbying for greater acceptance of diversity.

In the past, it would have been difficult and quite possibly dangerous for mixed marriage people to bring attention to themselves and their decisions to put love and commitment before tradition, but, less than three years ago, NIMMA's 'Mixed Emotions' book did just that.

Its success, its use in the Integrated Education sector and its impact on the local media broke new ground for what had been a taboo subject and paved the way for discussion among many of our young people. A sequel about the children of such mixed relationships was inevitable.

These individual stories, real life experiences in the words of the people themselves, speak of hope and courage, compromise and determination. They tell of good times and bad, of love and prejudice, of difference and division, but they also speak of family as a force for good, often against all the odds.

They will do much to separate fact from fiction, stretching back more than 50 years, to spark debate and to open minds and the brief 'History of Mixed Marriage in Ireland' included in this book should guide any reader to a fuller understanding of where we have been and where a shared future can take us.

Mohandas Gandhi, political and spiritual leader, declared that, "If we are to teach real peace in this world, we shall have to begin with the children" and, with that in mind, the mothers and fathers of the 'children' who contributed to this book, many of whom are pictured and quoted within, are to be congratulated for their openness and support. Their children enjoy the legacy of their trust and their bravery.

Our author, Paul McLaughlin, who has more than thirty years experience of interviewing in the private, public and voluntary sectors, describes himself as having 'been very fortunate to have met and worked with the brave people whose stories make up this book'. He said, "It is never easy in Northern Ireland to be different, to break the sectarian mould and to talk about it openly. Unfortunately as a society, we have not yet moved that far, but these folk have done it and done it for the benefit of others. I appreciate what they have given".

I echo those words and trust that the book will be an inspiration to all who read it.

Professor Pete Shirlow
Deputy Director of the Institute for Conflict Transformation and Social Justice
Queen's University Belfast

Introduction

Anonymous quotes and sayings are no less powerful for being coined first by unknowns. While the author may be lost in the mists of time, what was written can and does often continue to resonate down the years. We all have a favourite and compilations of quotations bustle with efforts from the unknown pen.

So it is with a quote that could have been conjured up just for this book. 'Children are great imitators, give them something great to imitate'. Our children, ranging in age from 16 to nearly 60, show how they have done just that and lived to tell the tale.

Making a mixed marriage in this country has never been easier, thanks in no small measure to the work of NIMMA over more than 40 years, but living that marriage continues to bring with it a range of problems unique to this part of the world. That 'baggage', for want of a better word, remains heavy in the carrying, despite progress and is, perhaps, the reason why less than a dozen volunteers have chosen to go public with their stories.

These are stories of courage, compromise and hope that are there for all to read, learn from and, perhaps, even imitate. I would like to thank all of our volunteer contributors for their courage and patience in taking part in this project, for their warmth of welcome into their lives and for the privilege of being allowed to share in their family experiences. It was humbling for me to say the least and I hope inspirational to our readers. I thank all those in NIMMA who tackled the almost thankless task of proof reading the material, particularly Ken and Maura Dunne.

And finally, a very big thank you to the Big Lottery Fund, the Esmee Fairbairn Foundation and St Anne's Cathedral Black Santa sit-out appeal for making the project possible and to Chris Madden for our cover photograph.

Paul McLaughlin
March 2015

A short history of mixed marriage in Ireland

By *Ken Dunn*,
Chairman of NIMMA

Introduction:

For the last century, marriage in Ireland between Protestants and Roman Catholics has been a very contentious issue, not fully understood by many. To understand and appreciate the depth of feeling about mixed marriage, it is helpful to look at the historical background. Since space is limited, the review will be brief with salient features highlighted. Some additional reading material is appended for those who want further details.

The early Church followed the marriage custom of the Roman Empire. The ring, the bride's veil and the exchange of promises that we know today all come from pagan Roman betrothal and marriage customs. The young couple announced their betrothal and on the appointed day there was a procession from the bride's parental home to the new matrimonial home for food and dance. The custom then developed that the procession would detour past the Church where the priest would come out, give a blessing and join the procession.

Such a system is very open to abuse – his word against hers. A man could walk out and journey a dozen villages away and start again! Thus, from the 11th century, the Church began to require that the couple exchanged their marriage vows before three witnesses; a priest and two lay people – todays bridesmaid and best man. This practice was formalised at the Council of Trent (1563) in a document called *Tametsi* (nevertheless). This was enforced only where it was promulgated. Ireland was very patchy.

Ulster	late sixteenth century
Tuam	1658 - 1745
Cashel	1785
Rest of Ireland	1827

Thus in the 264 years from 1563 to 1827 Ireland had time to develop its own approach to mixed marriage.

With the coming of the Reformation, we have 'mixed marriage', i.e. marriage between a Roman Catholic and a Protestant. Originally mixed marriage laws referred to marriage with a pagan and required that the children be Catholic. At the Reformation, the Protestants were considered pagans and the same should apply. In Europe, most countries followed the denomination of the ruling King or Prince.

In the Spanish Netherlands in the 1590s, Tametsi was used to persecute the Protestant population:

"The most effective weapon in eliminating the Protestants was the proclamation that marriages celebrated by Protestant pastors were null and void. The children thus became illegitimate and were automatically barred from all public office or honourable careers."[1]

Thus a decree, intended to eliminate a social evil, was now used to eliminate Protestants.

When the Spanish left and the Calvinists were in the majority, the Civil Law in Belgium and Holland required that a mixed marriage be performed before the Calvinist minister only. In 1741, Pope Benedict XIV recognised mixed marriages without Roman Catholic priests being present[2]. This was extended to Ireland by Pius VI in 1785 and reinforced in 1906 in the Decree Provida which stipulated that mixed marriage everywhere would be exempt and always remain valid when conducted before a protestant minister.

In the 1680s, when Louis XIV was persecuting the Huguenots as a preliminary to revoking the Edict of Nantes

"Mixed marriages were prohibited and children born of them were declared illegitimate and snatched from their parents to be brought up in the Catholic religion"[3]

Meanwhile we have the Penal Laws in Ireland. These were modelled on the French anti-Huguenot laws. Up to 1793, it was a capital offence for a Roman Catholic priest to officiate at a mixed marriage. The last hanging was in 1726. From 1793 to 1833 this was reduced to a fine of £5,000. At the time, the Roman Catholic Bishop of Ossory, later Archbishop of Dublin, John Troy said: "marriage between Protestants and Catholics is unlawful, wicked, and dangerous. The Penal Laws should not be repealed because they act as a deterrent".[4]

Thus, we see mixed marriages are **equally popular on both sides**!

The *Tametsi* decree was published in parts of Tuam Archdiocese in 1658, in other parts in 1745, but Galway city was an exception. It was ruled by a Warden in almost total independence from the Archbishop. Mixed marriages were considered in the city to be valid whether preformed in the Protestant or Catholic Church. Furthermore, no promise about the children was required. This somewhat confused situation led throughout Ireland to what historians call the *Galway Convention*, where the boys followed the father's and the girls the mother's denomination.[5] This ensured that land and property did not change denomination.

In 1850 the Synod of Thurles imposed on Ireland the equivalent of the future *Ne Temere* decree. A mixed marriage (a) needed a Papal Dispensation and (b) required that all the children be brought up as Roman Catholics. Both partners were required to make the promise verbally and in writing before witnesses. However, the regulations of Thurles were widely ignored. Furthermore, in 1852, the English Roman Catholic Bishops took the view that the dispensation should be from a parish priest and not Rome. When this was confirmed by Rome in 1853, the practice was widely taken up in Ireland. In 1858, Rome decreed that mixed marriages could not take place in church.

However, at the end of the nineteenth century the Vatican was on a 'tidy up' of all its legislation and one result was the *Ne Temere* (not casually) decree of 19th April 1908. Now all marriages in Ireland, including mixed marriages, would be subject to the Tridentine Law. The result of this legislation was that both partners (a) promised to bring up all the children as Roman Catholic, (b) the Catholic partner worked to convert the other, and (c) the marriage could not take place in Church and with no ceremony only the exchange of vows. Hungary and Germany were exempt until 1917. The decree was then universally applied on publication of the new Code of Canon Law [1917].

Ne Temere was enthusiastically applied by the Irish clergy. At the same time, we have civil unrest, a new border and civil war in Ireland. Dr Garrett Fitzgerald has shown, wearing his statistician's hat, that *Ne Temere* was the prime factor in reducing the Protestant population of the Irish Republic by 80%. At independence, there was an initial exodus followed by the second phase of attrition using *Ne Temere*. Contrary to Roman Canon Law, this was often applied retrospectively and marriages of long-standing were broken up. We can compare, in the same period, the 60% increase in the Roman Catholic population of Northern Ireland. Dr Fitzgerald asked the Irish Bishops to request Rome for a relaxation of *Ne Temere*, but they refused. Professor Oliver Rafferty SJ, Maynooth, has said that one of the Roman Catholic Church's most remarkable self-inflicted wounds was *Ne Temere*. It gave further evidence that Home Rule was indeed Rome Rule[6].

This is perhaps best understood by looking at the McCann case. Agnes and Alexander McCann were married in Antrim Presbyterian Church in May 1908. They moved to Belfast where Agnes worshipped at Townsend Street Presbyterian Church. By summer 1910, they had two children, Joseph and Mary. Alexander was informed by a parish priest that he was 'living in sin' and must marry in front of a priest. Agnes considered that they were properly married already and would not agree to this. In October 1910, Alexander and the two children disappeared. A distracted Mrs McCann roamed the streets of Belfast asking all she met if they had seen her babies. The case was widely publicised by her minister the Rev William Corkey. This was the first major outing of *Ne Temere* in Ulster and there were riots in the streets of Belfast, major public protest meetings in Belfast, Edinburgh, Glasgow, London, Dublin and Australia, Canada and New Zealand. Questions were asked in the House of Commons and a debate was held in the House of Lords (1910). We now know that Alexander and the two children were assisted to move to the USA and settled near Pittsburgh. Agnes never again saw or heard from her husband or children.

Prior to 1910, the Presbyterian General Assembly had 30% of its members in favour of Home Rule, after the McCann case just 4%! The future Church of Ireland Archbishop of both Dublin and Armagh John Gregg was then Dean in Cork. He said:

"The Protestant is to surrender every right of conscience that he possesses, except that he is graciously allowed to remain a Protestant himself, though he must submit to reasonable efforts to make a Romanist of him."

"If you hope to arrive at any reconciliation with Protestants, if you want to make even the thought of Home Rule not a nightmare to us, you will revolt against this portion of the decree: you will protest against it, you will drum it out of Cork, out of Ireland."

"It did look as if the barriers were becoming less unpassable; this uncalled-for decree from Italy has thrown national concord back by a hundred years."

"How can you expect us to trust ourselves to you? The decree is an attack on Irish Unity and can only make Protestants more irreconcilable to the idea of Home Rule"[8].

The hostility of the Orange Order to mixed marriage is overt and widely recognised. In 1916 the Grand Master of the Order, Colonel Wallace, declared that "...the decree is final proof that Home Rule is Rome Rule."[8]

A member entering a mixed marriage must leave the order if any of the children are brought up as Roman Catholics despite the claim that the Order stands for religious and civil liberty. This attitude is, of course, simply the mirror image of *Ne Temere*.

To quote Archbishop Donald Coggan of Canterbury (1967) referring to mixed marriage "there can be few points of contact which are fraught with more potential opportunity – either for ecumenical advance or for discord". **In Ireland we usually opt for the discord**.

Even in 1941 Bishop Mageean of Down and Connor, at a Confirmation service in St Teresa's parish on the Glen Road, declared mixed marriage evil and boasted that in a neighbouring diocese no mixed marriage had taken place under four successive Bishops.[9]

In 1957, an Interchurch couple, Sheila and Sean Cloney, living in Fethard-on-Sea in south Wexford were visited by the local Roman Catholic clergy and informed that the children "will go to the Catholic school". The Church of Ireland wife disagreed with such an edict and took herself and the children to Belfast and on to Scotland. The local Catholics were convinced that a mere woman could not have managed this without help from her Protestant neighbours and relatives. They then instigated a boycott of the Protestant owned shops and farms. Even the elderly lady giving piano lessons had her young Catholic pupils withdrawn.

The main boycott lasted for five months, from the end of April 1957, although many local Catholics continued the boycott for many years. The local Roman Catholic Bishop completely supported the boycott and Bishop Browne of Galway preached on the virtues of the boycott. The local Knights of Saint Columbanus and Gaelic Athletic Association policed and enforced the main boycott. De Valera eventually intervened to condemn the action, but again this outworking of the Irish Roman Catholic clergy's take on *Ne Temere* was being used to reinforce the message that Home Rule was indeed Rome Rule. Some readers may have seen the movie 'A Love Divided' made of this event.[10]

On a lighter note, Justin Keating, a future Dublin Labour Party Minister for Industry and Commerce, as a protest would go with a friend to Fethard to shop in Protestant shops and then to local pubs to purchase Jameson whiskey or Guinness. They would then say to the locals "you would boycott an elderly Protestant piano teacher, but you are drinking the Protestant drink". A swift exit usually followed!

Finally, in this sorry tale, we have the Tilson case in Dublin 1950. They were a mixed marriage couple recently working in Dublin. She ran off with another man leaving him with the three children. With no child minder available, he put the children into a Protestant Children's Home until such times as he had child-care in place. She demanded the children be brought up as good Catholics like herself and went to the High Court. The judge ruled that the pre-nuptial agreement overruled the common law principle that the husband was the head of the family with the right to decide the religious upbringing. Judge Gavin Duffy ruled that the Irish Constitution articles 41, 42, and 44 gave precedent to Roman Canon Law over civil law. Of course, it was appealed to the Supreme Court where 4 of the 5 judges agreed with Judge Duffy's conclusion. The fifth, Judge Black, was the only Protestant judge on the Supreme Court.[11] This ruling undoubtedly gave comfort to the Roman Catholic Bishops when they refused to report child sexual abuse by their clergy to the civil authority.

Things eased a little in 1966 when Rome issued *Matrimonii Sacramentum* which removed the requirement that the Catholic partner must "work prudently for the conversion of the non-Catholic spouse". This unchristian attitude to Interchurch marriage was recognised by Bishop Willie Walsh of Killaloe (1994-2010) in the Furrow 1997. "It has been a long journey from the sadness and isolation forced on many a young couple who wanted to share their life and love in marriage but who belonged to different Christian traditions. It has been a long journey from that sadness and isolation to the joyfulness of today's Interchurch marriage witnessed by ministers of both denominations. And if one is to appropriate blame for the pain and hurt, I believe that the principle fault was on our side – to our eyes today the Roman Catholic Ne Temere decree was indeed contrary to the spirit of Christian generosity and love. I feel that many of us would want to apologise to and ask forgiveness from our non-Roman Catholic brethren for that pain and hurt."

I have not discussed the behaviour of the Protestant Churches in Ireland. This is because, with one exception, they have not been proactive, but rather reactive. The one occasion is the Anglican Roman Catholic International Commission [ARCIC] report on Marriage (1967) that was co-chaired by Archbishop George Simms of Armagh[12]. Their early reports were partially incorporated into new legislation arising from the Second Vatican Council *Matrimonia Mixta* (1970). This now permitted the marriage in Church and required that only the Roman Catholic partner need promise to do all, within his or her power **within the marriage**, to bring the children up as Roman Catholic.

Next in our historical survey is 1974 and the formation of the Northern Ireland Mixed Marriage Association [NIMMA]. This was the result of a weekend conference organised by Corrymeela for those interested, involved, or hoping to be involved in mixed marriage. The association developed four main aims:

1.	Self help – pastoral care. With a few honourable exceptions among the clergy this did not exist elsewhere;

2.	Provision of advice and information to other couples;

3.   Help for the clergy to fully understand mixed marriage;

4.   To influence the local community's attitudes.

From 1995 to 2004, we were part-funded by the NI Community Relations Council with an office in Bryson House, Belfast. However, CRC then decided that NIMMA were no longer needed and funding ended. We have been funded since 2005 by the Dublin Department of Foreign Affairs Anglo-Irish Division's Reconciliation Fund.

There are many **sister organisations** around the world: England and Wales; Ireland; France; Germany; Italy; Austria; Switzerland; New Zealand; Australia; USA; Canada. All but France and Switzerland call themselves Associations of Interchurch Families. The modern **definitions** commonly used for mixed marriages include: both, one or neither partner practising. When both are practising, they are referred to as an Interchurch couple. NIMMA deliberately kept the options open for all to join. So by our definition, two humanists from perceived Protestant/Roman Catholic backgrounds are in a mixed marriage.

One unexpected outcome has been the **international dimension**. An international conference has been held every two years since 1980; hosted by NIMMA in 1982 and 1990. This has led to NIMMA having influence in Rome. The international committee has met the Pontifical Council in Rome to discuss the way forward and further meetings are planned. The Council have asked that initially local Bishops Conferences should be approached to obtain practical changes in their areas. NIMMA continues to argue for changes in the approach to baptism, Eucharistic sharing and education.

The Position Today:

I want to look at the influence mixed marriage couples have had on the Churches and will first quote Bishop Samuel Poyntz, at that time C of I Bishop of Cork, at an Interchurch meeting in Ballymascanlon in 1984 "It must be encouragement to many involved in the sometimes lonely tension of a two-church marriage to realise that over the years the Churches have not managed to change the couple, rather have the couple done much to change the characteristic attitudes of the Churches". This is most clearly seen in the Roman Catholic Directory on Mixed Marriages in Ireland (1983)[13]. NIMMA made written and oral submissions and six of our eight proposals were accepted. Our views were championed by Cardinal O'Fee who freely recognised the harm done by Ne Temere.

The agreed proposals were:

1: Joint Pastoral Care from both clergy acting together.
2: The appointment of Diocesan specialists.
   This has been a great success.
3: The wedding should take place in the bride's Church –
   the social norm.
4: There would not normally be a nuptial mass.
   To declare the couple united in marriage and then
   disunited at the Eucharist is theological nonsense.
5: Both clergy to be present at the wedding, robed
   and taking an active part.
6: A proper understanding of the Promise.

The two proposals refused were Eucharistic sharing and concelebrated baptism. I will expand on only one, the Promise. This is the most contentious and the one that has caused the most damage to community relations in the past 100 years.

The original promise read:

"I declare that I am resolved, as God's law demands, to preserve my Catholic faith, and to avoid all danger of falling away from it. Moreover, I sincerely undertake and I will, as God's law requires, do every thing possible, as far as in me lies, to have all of the children of our marriage baptised and brought up in the Catholic faith."

This has undergone some change and the Catholic partner is now asked:

"Do you promise to do what you can within the unity of your marriage to have all of the children of your marriage baptised and brought up in the Catholic faith."

This is more understandable and much more user friendly, but what does it mean?

The Directory its self states in section 8.1 that: "The religious upbringing of the children is the joint responsibility of both parents. The obligations of the Catholic party do not, and cannot, cancel out or in any way call into question, the conscientious duties of the other party."

Section 8.5 continues " Nonetheless, the decision about the education of the children does not belong to the Catholic party alone. The actual circumstances of the marriage form the context in which this obligation must be carried out and these circumstances are bound to vary considerably. The possibility exists that the Catholic will be in a situation where some or all of the children are brought up in the denomination of the other party."

Thus **now** the upbringing of the children is the **sole responsibility of the parents** to do what is right for them in their marriage. A major grievance has now been removed.

We also need to look at the wider international scene. While the general theological aspects are similar the world over, the living conditions do differ considerably. In Northern Ireland, we have 90% segregated housing, 94% segregated schools, separate teacher training colleges, separate games and separate dances/pubs. These conditions do not exist anywhere else in the world, though they once did in the White-controlled South Africa and, of course, in some southern states of the United States. This has resulted in NIMMA being involved, in association with Housing Trusts and the NI Housing Executive, to provide reserved housing in neutral areas for mixed marriage couples - an alien concept to the rest of the world. NIMMA's continual lobbying and our representation on the NIHE Housing Advisory Committee has helped bring about the 'Shared Neighbourhood Programme', which has developed 30 shared neighbourhoods across the Province over a three year period.

[Shared neighbourhoods are where people choose to live with others, regardless of religion or race, in an area that is safe and welcoming to all. NIMMA's determination to pursue, for 20 years, shared social housing grew out of our experiences in providing advice and practical help to couples facing intimidation.]

To obtain housing or employment, the applicant is generally required to state their perceived religion. But the children of Interchurch couples would argue that they are not **either** but **both**. Housing associations and the Civil Service have not found this a comfortable concept. Indeed, refusal to tick one box or to tick both boxes means that a Civil Service job application will be refused. Is this the way to a shared future? As this was being written, the NIHE application form was changed to include a tick box for dual church membership!

Many people would consider that with the present state of religious practice, mixed marriages are no longer a problem. Unfortunately, this is not the case. We still have our dinosaur clergy and laity.

For example in the recent past we have had the problem of:

(1) A couple visiting the parish priest to discuss their wedding plans. When he discovered that the non-Roman Catholic would not be converting on marriage, he declared the couple 'evil' and asked them to leave
(2) A Church of Ireland rector refused to discuss a mixed marriage with one of his parishioners
(3) Community relations are not good west of the Bann, but sympathetic Roman Catholic clergy working there have

asked us to help the Presbyterian clergy deal positively with mixed marriage couples

Laity continue to be a problem, with many demanding that the grandchildren be baptised into their denomination irrespective of the wishes of the couple. In Ireland, both north and south, land and property have often acquired denominational labels and couples are told that they will not inherit the farm or business if the marriage goes ahead.

Lest anyone think that I have been pessimistic, this is not the case. We have made much progress over the PAST 40 years as a reading of the stories in this book will demonstrate. The number of mixed relationships in Northern Ireland is increasing steadily, with more mixing thanks to fair employment legislation, Integrated Schools and a desire by most of the wider community for a shared future.

Before the Belfast Agreement, the number of couples calling NIMMA went up because most politicians do not lead, but follow the electorate. Thus the rate of new mixed relationships is a good measure of the success of Reconciliation in the community.

Indeed we cannot and will not have true peace until all can feel free to inter-marry if they so wish.

K.Dunn
Chairman, NIMMA

Further details on mixed relationships and the work of NIMMA can be obtained from
our web site **www.nimma.org.uk**
or by email to nimma@nireland.com
or by phone to our office 028 9023 5444

References

1. *History of the Belgians*, A de Meeus, Praeger New York 1962.

2. Mixed marriage and Irish politics: the effect of *Ne Temere*, Eoin de Bhaldraithe, Studies, Autumn 1988.

3. *The Church in the Seventeenth Century*, Daniel-Rops, London: Dent 1963.

4. *Priests and People in Pre-Famine Ireland, 1780-1845*, SJ Connolly. Gill and Macmillan, 2001.

5. *The Wardens of Galway*, RJ Kelly, J of the Roy Soc Antiquarians, Ireland 1896.

6. *Catholicism in Ulster* 1603-1983, Oliver P Rafferty SJ. Gill and Macmillan, 1994.

7. *Glad did I live*, William Corkey, The Belfast News-Letter Ltd, Belfast, 1962

8. *The Ne Temere Decree*, JF Gregg. APCK, Dublin, 1911

9. *On this day*, E Phoenix. The Irish News, June 17, 2010

10. *The Fethard-on-Sea Boycott*, T Fanning. The Collins Press, 2010.

11. *Church and State in Modern Ireland*, JH Whyte. Gill and Macmillan, 1980.

12. *George Otto Simms*, L Whiteside. Colin Smythe Ltd, 1990.

13. *Directory on Mixed Marriage*, Irish Episcopal Conference. Veritas Dub. 1983.

Further Reading

Beyond Tolerance: The Challenge of Mixed Marriage, Ed Fr M Hurley, Chapman London, 1975.

Two Churches One Love, Rev A Heron. APCK 1977.

Mixed Marriage in Ireland, A companion for those involved or about to be involved in a mixed marriage, NIMMA, 3rd edition 2003.

Interchurch Marriage in Ireland, A &W Odling-Smee. Catalyst, 2001.

For the impact of *Ne Temere* on Ireland see
Fr Ralph, G O'Donovan. Macmillan and Co London, 1913
Waiting, G O'Donovan. Macmillan and Co London, 1914

ACKNOWLEDGEMENT:

Publication of this book, which is the natural sequel to our first book about mixed marriage couples, 'Mixed Emotions', would not have been possible without the invaluable support of The Big Lottery Fund and our core funder the Esmee Fairbairn Foundation. NIMMA gratefully acknowledges their contributions.

Chris Madden

Cover photographer Chris Madden works as a 'very busy' recruitment consultant in the City of London. He was born in Belfast in 1993 to a Catholic father and a Protestant mother, baptised a Catholic, but attended both the RC Church and Baptist church in Carrickfergus for many years.

He went to an integrated nursery, playgroup and primary school, Acorn Integrated Primary School, before going on to Ulidia Integrated College.

In 2008, he was awarded a full three year scholarship to the prestigious St Albans School in Washington DC - a scholarship funded by an Irish-American, Jack McDonnell, who is a strong supporter of integrated education.

Chris graduated from St Albans in 2011 and went to study War Studies and History at King's College London. From 2012-2014, he worked as a parliamentary assistant to Alliance Party MP Naomi Long in the House of Commons. He has been a member of the party since he was 14 years of age.

He graduated from King's with First Class Honours last year, before taking up his job in the City. Chris describes it as 'frenetic and stimulating and my biggest challenge so far'.

The cover picture was taken during the London Olympic Games in 2012.

Contents

Contents

Healing the Hurt

Anne Townsend is a former social worker and part-time member of the Ulster Defence Regiment from the picturesque village of Kesh in the Fermanagh Lakelands. She remembers her childhood with fondness but blames 'The Troubles' for family and community divisions.

I am the eldest of nine children born to a Protestant father from Ederney and a Roman Catholic mother from Irvinestown. We were brought up in my father's denomination: that was Mummy's and Daddy's joint decision. They had met as teenagers, only seventeen, back in the early 1950s and, despite the religious climate of the time had fallen in love: to such an extent that soon mum was attending Church of Ireland services and preparing for marriage outside her own denomination. No easy choice in those days, but mum was strong-willed and determined, despite her parents being dead and having only one sister living this side of the Irish Sea, and she even faced down a disciplinary visit from the local Roman Catholic hierarchy.

They had expressed their disapproval of the match, particularly the fact that it was going to take place in a Protestant church and told her that any children of the marriage would be regarded as 'bastards'. They were sent off with a flea in their respective ears and mum and dad went on to make a civil marriage - ironically, in the Republic of Ireland.

Mummy kept in close contact with her Roman Catholic sister, my aunt, and friends in the years after her marriage and got on with her life. She was the type of woman who would not be told what to do and was all the better for it I'm sure. She showed that strength of character in many ways, none more familiar to me now than her determination that we children should go to church regularly, which we did. It's funny now, but back then my sisters and I were the only girls in the Church of Ireland church on St Patrick's Day with green ribbons in their hair! A little bit of ecumenism on the feast of the patron saint.

Relations between Roman Catholics and Protestants were good in this area back then. We lived cheek-by-jowl with our religious counterparts and got on well. Each year, Catholic farmers would milk the cows of their Orangemen neighbours to let them get to the Twelfth celebrations at the field and the Hibernians even loaned their bass drum to the local lodge for a parade. Land was always a bone of contention, of course, and neither denomination would have sold an acre to other than 'their own'.

I was probably about the age of nine or ten before I was even aware of my parents' mixed marriage, or indeed understood much about the terms Catholic and Protestant. I had gone to a mixed religion primary school and it was there one afternoon that another girl and I had a tiff. I remember becoming very upset as she shouted 'Your mummy's a turncoat'. I thought that this was some awful affliction that had befallen my mother. Not wishing to approach her I asked my grandmother what it meant. She informed me that my parents were of different beliefs and that was the end of that. It was not discussed again for many years. Amazingly, the girl who had brought it to my attention was herself the product of a mixed marriage.

My mother and my father's mother were two of a kind - strong opinionated women that spoke their minds. Like all families, there could be friction and I well remember my Granny referring to Mummy as 'a black so and so' when she was in a bad mood. The 'black' referred to her dark, Irish looks. I'm not sure what she would have said if she'd heard Mummy singing the occasional rebel song - nothing printable for certain.

My siblings and I went to Sunday school, were confirmed and subsequently went to church each Sunday. Mummy insisted. My friends, both in and out of primary school, prior to secondary school, were of both persuasions. It was not until secondary school that I began to realise that things about religion were not that simple. I had Roman Catholic cousins, but religion was never mentioned. Then 'The Troubles' started and even though I was brought up to respect every one irrespective of their religion everything changed. People changed and not for the better. Sadly, politics go hand-in-hand with religion in this part of the world and 30 years of violence and death were disastrous for community and even family relations. In an atmosphere of fear and suspicion, contact was broken off with my Roman Catholic aunt and cousins. People kept to their own and that meant their own denomination. It was only with the coming of the peace agreement that people began to speak again.

I had been in the security forces like others in my family and we were naturally suspicious of the 'other' side. I also had family who were well-known Republicans. It was a surreal sort of situation. Sad, but that's just the way it was. A divided society along religious lines – family or no family. Things improved afterwards of course. Some of my Catholic cousins came to Daddy's funeral and the Royal British Legion Club afterwards, but things can never be the same. There's an innocence that was destroyed and we can't get that back.

I met my husband, Pete, while working in England. He's from outside Southampton and even after living here all these years he doesn't understand the emotional pull of religious division. It came as a culture shock to him and we determined that our children should have as balanced a view as was possible. I went to that little country primary school that taught both denominations long before the days of integrated education, and I sent two of my children there as well. I think that it is the natural way for children, regardless of their denomination, to be educated together. It is certainly the only way forward for this country.

My family, down three generations, has been mixed and boys and girls have followed their hearts and chosen tolerance over tribalism. Three of my siblings went on to have mixed marriages and there have been more mixed relationships with my own children. I cannot say that I have been more respectful or tolerant with those of a different persuasion because of my background as my opinions have been influenced by what has been happening in Northern Ireland during particularly dark years. Mind you, I have not allowed my opinions to impact negatively on my children: my grandson is from a mixed relationship and my son has been in one for more than ten years. I think Pete and I have done okay in that respect.

I think about my own situation some times. I think I'm not really one thing or the other: that I don't really belong to either side, and maybe that is a good thing. I don't know. It can be confusing. I can remember resenting my mother for having been a Roman Catholic, especially when I was teenager at the height of 'The Troubles'. I guess mixed families were a little embarrassing at that time. Forty years ago, Kesh would have been regarded as a Protestant village – a 'black hole' was how I heard it described many times. But today, thanks to the peace and more and more mixed marriages and relationships here, we are a more diverse and less-divided community.

I have never been anti-Catholic, thank God. I am anti-Republican, but, unlike many so-called Protestants, I can see the difference between the two. I don't love my Roman Catholic nephews and nieces any less because of their religion and I long for the day when, thanks to full integration in education, that children see each other as children - not Catholics or Protestants - just children.

My mother suffered 30 years of separation from her family because of the impact of the violence here and if there was one thing I would like to see for the future it is a Northern Ireland where people take people for who they are, not what they are. Sadly, we can't get back those years, but we can start to heal some of the hurt.

Anne with her mum and sisters

A Recipe for Happiness

Louise is a 29-year-old piano teacher from Belfast and former tour guide at Crumlin Road gaol. She lives near the village of Hannahstown on the slopes of the Black Mountain. The youngest of three children, her memories of growing up the child of a mixed marriage are as clear as the vista of her native city from her kitchen window.

I am the child of a mixed marriage. Sometimes that statement seems completely absurd: both my parents are white, Christian and from Northern Ireland, but the justification is in that final element - Northern Ireland.

I was twelve-years-old when the Belfast Peace Agreement was signed, was in no way oblivious to the 'Troubles' growing up in West Belfast, but coming from a 'mixed marriage' may have provided me with a perspective different to that of my Catholic school friends. Things weren't as 'black and white' or as 'green and orange' to me as they may have been to other children: Protestants weren't those strange people that lived in 'their' part of the city and had beliefs so different to mine. How could they be? My father was a Protestant.

My parents married in 1973; they had met while working in the Civil Service. Until they'd announced their engagement my mother had had a good relationship with my father's Church-of-Ireland parents, but the commitment of marriage changed that. My paternal grandfather didn't support the decision and neither of my father's parents attended the wedding, which was held in a Roman Catholic church and blessed later by a Church of Ireland minister.

I'm sure that absence was hurtful and it's difficult to fathom fully why this petty disapproval transpired. It certainly had nothing to do with politics – my grandfather was a Dublin Irishman and my grandmother was proud of her Donegal inheritance. It was about religion and I'll never understand why minor differences in spiritual belief caused such discontent. Perhaps, like a lot of Northern Irish nuances, it was about labels.

My father continued to see his parents, but acceptance was never extended to my mother. Eight years passed and one sunny afternoon when they were spending the weekend on the coast at Magilligan my father called his parents who lived close by in Derry City. He told them that he was nearby with his family and that they were welcome to join him. They did and this was the first time that they met their grandchildren – Stephen, eight, and Niamh, three. By the time I was born in 1985 visits to Derry were regular, full of happy memories and enjoyed by everyone. Perhaps time healed old wounds, but I certainly believe children put things in perspective. We were christened Catholic and my grandfather certainly didn't love us any less because of our religion.

So, I had Catholic aunts, uncles and cousins and Protestant aunts, uncles and cousins. Meanwhile, on the news the incessant media reports describing the conflict between 'Protestants and Catholics' reinforced the perception of complete opposition between the two. Was I the only child of a mixed marriage? Perhaps if I'd gone to an integrated Primary School, I'd not have thought so, but they were few and far between in 1989 .

One day in my Catholic all-girls school, a classmate asked me why my daddy never went to Mass. She remarked that she saw me every Sunday with my mum, but never my dad. I thought for a moment before I remembered the answer.

"My daddy is a Protestant," I said matter-of-factly.
She gawped with concern, before blurting it out to the rest of my class.
"Her daddy is a Protestant!"
Gasp after gasp. Mouths hung open. Whispers ensued.

I didn't cry or go back on my word as you might think a nine-year-old would. Instead, I laughed: how silly these girls were thinking my daddy being a Protestant was a big deal!

Of course, back then we went on EMU trips (Education for Mutual Understanding) with Orangefield Primary School. The beautiful thing about children is that they'd rather look for compatibility than differences in potential friends. My all-girls class was so agitated about spending time with boys that we almost forgot they were Protestant. Anyway, I had plenty of opportunity to spend time with Protestants – my own cousins.

When it came to family, differences like religion barely mattered. We shared the same grandparents – what was more important than that? In fact, differences were hardly discussed at all and, when they were, it was interesting rather than conflicting. One evening when my cousins were over for dinner, my mother went upstairs to find one of them dressed in my sister's old First Communion dress. She hadn't received Holy Communion or the opportunity to wear a big white dress and veil – so we decided to have one for her and dressed her up accordingly!

I continued my education in an all-girls Catholic secondary school, and when I was sixteen I decided to apply for the Spirit of Eniskillen. It was a youth-led charity that took people from different cultural backgrounds to find areas of commonality. Many of my friends had gone on these trips and enjoyed them, but my application wasn't successful. Because I was already from a 'mixed marriage' the interviewer couldn't understand how I would benefit from the trip. Once again, I felt like an outsider.

I hadn't been thinking about what I would take from the experience – it was about what I could give. I wanted young people to see that it's not just Protestant or Catholic: that plenty of children come from a happily mixed background, that we weren't outsiders. For me it wasn't about team-building trips away or weekend workshops, but rather the example of lifetime partnerships that blur the 'boundaries' completely and show the way to a shared future.

Northern Ireland is different now than it was twenty years ago. Belfast is blossoming nicely with restaurants and wine bars and a vibrant night life that brings together people of all sorts. Things have come on leaps and bounds and attitudes have changed massively since that evening in 1995 when I stood at Belfast City Hall with thousands of optimistic citizens to watch President Bill Clinton cast a spell over the city. It felt good then and still does.

With every new generation comes more acceptance of diversity. Protestant and Catholic labels are becoming less distinct as the country welcomes new nationalities, cultures and religions and what used to seem so important is fading into the past. Of course, not everyone is as optimistic as I am. My brother Stephen left Belfast for university across the water more than 20 years ago - he couldn't wait to get away - has married and has a family and a new life there. I speak with him regularly on the 'phone and sadly, he still feels the same. He didn't get the chance to see how things have changed and are continuing to change and remains downbeat about Northern Ireland.

I look to the future and the belief that we have the commonsense and humour to face it together.

Ironically, having been raised the Catholic child of a mixed marriage, I'm now in a relationship with a Protestant. We have no problems with religion or about religion, it isn't that important to us, but, unlike when my parents got married and my father was coerced into making promises about the denomination in which his children should be raised – he never did by the way - we know we can rely on the support of NIMMA if we need it. If we do get married, I'm not sure I'd ever call it a 'mixed' one anyway. After all, it will have the same ingredients that went into my parent's marriage and we'll just be repeating the same recipe. Not with the label a 'mixed marriage', but, hopefully, rather a 'happy marriage'.

Louise's mum and dad on their Wedding day

A Lucky Guy

Eoin Trainor is an 18-year-old 'A level' student from the suburbs of South Belfast. Taking time out from bashing an electronic drum kit or a hockey ball for his local club, Eoin, a senior scout with the Carryduff troop, reflects on his luck of the 'Northern Irish'.

I was born on July 11th and each year my birthday is festooned with bunting and flags. Just a coincidence? Of course, but with Grandads called Billy and Paddy, I have a foot firmly in both camps in this wee country. What a lucky guy I am. I say that with as much humility as a teenager can muster, because I fully realise that I have been and continue to be lucky. I don't feel particularly special being a mixed marriage kid, but I do feel special being me and being able to appreciate that I have a share in the two cultures here, and even luckier to have parents and grandparents who are good people.

Life's all about people when you get right down to it. I suppose that that sounds a bit naïve, but if I can't be idealistic at 18, when can I be? I'm in a good place in my life and I look forward to even better times ahead when our society is less polarised and people take a large pinch of tolerance before making judgements on others. I did say I was idealistic!

My home is in Carryduff to the south of Belfast. It is the kind of place that all of the country should be like. No disrespect to the Shankill or the Falls, but our village has all that's best about Northern Ireland. It is a mixed area where people respect diversity and get on with their lives without bigotry and hatred. And it's fun. I can beat the hell out of my electronic drum kit and not bother a soul except myself and my hearing through a set of headphones; I can play hockey for the Saintfield club, get beaten regularly and still have a laugh with the best mates around. Winning is a bonus we don't get often, but you can't have everything, even at 18.

My folks featured in the first NIMMA book and that got me thinking about their backgrounds more than anything else. I'm sure they had difficult times back then, what with 'The Troubles', coming from very different traditions, even from distant parts of the city, but they too were lucky to have families that showed acceptance and understanding and they've carried on that shared tradition with my brother and sisters. They both come from working-class backgrounds, are proud of their roots and don't think that only middle-class people are capable of tolerance. There are good people everywhere, but they need a chance to have a future. Politicians take note!

I'm now an 'A level' student at Wellington College in Belfast, but I've come through the Integrated system and I can't speak too highly of it. I went to an integrated primary school and, thinking back, I suppose there were a lot of mixed marriage kids there. Wellington is just like that: mixed ethnically and from a religious point of view, but religion just doesn't come into it. Is there the occasional bigot? Yes, unfortunately, there are idiots everywhere. Is anyone listening to him? No, there is enough good-natured banter and craic to drown out all that nonsense. As far as I'm concerned, difference doesn't matter. I have friends that I like regardless of whether they are Catholics or Protestants, black or white. They are what they are, there is no THEM and US in my world.

Identity is important, of course. We all need to feel part of something bigger. I see myself as Northern Irish. That about sums up the mixture of British and Irish cultures that are the backdrop to my life. I feel just as comfortable playing hockey as I do cheering on my local hurling team near our holiday house in Donegal. I have the best of both worlds.

Religion doesn't play a big part in my life at the minute anyway. Maybe that's normal for someone my age. I was baptised Catholic and made my First Communion and Confirmation, but I don't think of religion in those terms. I do think about God and the afterlife – not all the time mind you – and I like to think that there isn't a right or a wrong way to approach God. Two thousand years of Christianity can probably be likened to just as many years of Chinese Whispers and a lot has been distorted to the extent that faith is less about love and more about division than it was ever meant to be.

The real issues today should not be based around religion and parades and flags and languages. Education, particularly integrated education, health and jobs and opportunities for young people should be top of the politicians' agenda. It's vital that the youth of this country stay in this country. I hope to go to university here if I'm lucky enough to qualify and I'm working hard to that end, but I know how fortunate I am to be in that position and to be helped and encouraged at home. Further down the line is hard to see, but, at some stage, I would like to use my experience of media studies to get a job in that area. Perhaps, production and behind the scenes work, but who knows? Long-term, I want to be happy and continue to be as balanced as I can be. I've had a better start than many, with folks that are proud of their backgrounds, but not afraid to break with tradition. They've also taught me to look for compromise rather than conflict. That seems the sensible thing to do and a lot less painful in the long run.

If I had a motto, it could be 'Have fun and try your best. Don't hurt anyone and try, even just a little, to see the other person's point of view'. I'm lucky because I've been given the chance to live this way for a very long time. I'd like others to have that too.

Eoin's mum and dad dressed for dinner

My Side of the Fence

David, 57, is a former officer in the Royal Ulster Constabulary who now runs a pub in the West of Scotland. He is a married father of two whose love of golf has seen him move to live on the edge of a links course.

When I was a schoolboy, there wasn't a single day that I can remember that I didn't try to hide the fact that my mother was a Roman Catholic. That seems absurd after all these years, absurd and very sad, but it was a major factor in my early life in the 1960s in a small town like Enniskillen. I was conscious of the 'Catholic thing' from very early on and like most children I didn't want to be different from my school friends, so I kept my secret to myself as much as I could. I don't come from a prejudiced family background on either side – far from it if the truth be told – but 'being different' invited attention and bullying and no-one wants that - particularly not a young boy.

My late mother, Kathleen, the source of my secret if you like, came from a very well-known family, the McDermotts, from the staunchly nationalist border village of Roslea in Co Fermanagh. They were a big family, popular in sporting and musical circles and I can still remember my mother's beautiful singing voice doing more than justice to a ballad or two. I'm sure that any musical ability I have comes from her.

My father's background was in the Church of Ireland, but with complications. Well, it wouldn't be Northern Ireland if there weren't complications. He was James and had been born on the island of Enniskillen right in the centre of the town. James served with the local Fire Brigade for all of his working life and was well-known and well-liked in the community. His years of service to that community were recognised officially when he received the British Empire Medal in 1977.

My father had been born into a Protestant family, but a miscarriage of justice at the local Model secondary school, when one of his two brothers was beaten for a breach of discipline that had nothing to do with him, led to my grandfather, a man of principle, having words with the headmaster and removing the boys from the school the same day. Amazingly, because this was during the 1930s, he enrolled the three lads at St Michael's, the Roman Catholic school that was run by the Irish Christian Brothers. It was a rare and radical move for the time, maybe for any time, but I'm sure it gave the lads a broader perspective than the majority of their segregated schoolmates. It also meant that they got a free period every time it came to Religious Instruction.

My mother trained as a nurse at Belfast's Royal Victoria Hospital and somehow, I'm not sure how, the nurse and the fireman, who was 18 years her senior, began courting and eventually married in St Macartin's Church of Ireland Cathedral. My mother's family, who were devout Roman Catholics, despite the Ne Temere decree, do not appear to have objected unduly and it was a 'normal' family wedding.

One of my mother's sisters also made a mixed marriage with a Protestant, but it would appear that most of the family's disapproval was directed at the sister who married an Englishman! I don't know what religion he was, but being English was enough to warrant family disfavour.

Family life for us continued to mean close relations with both sides and though my mother and father decided to raise us as members of the Church of Ireland I don't recall any difference made by Roman Catholic aunts, uncles or cousins. Both my Catholic grandparents were deceased and maybe, in a strange kind of way, that made things a bit easier. I do remember that my mother was as zealous as any Catholic mother about her children and made us go to church every Sunday.

My summer holidays were spent at an aunt's house in the St James area of West Belfast and that was where I was when 'The Troubles' broke out in August of 1969. You couldn't make it up. At night, my Catholic cousins and I listened for the gunfire and explosions and watched the flames as cars and buildings were set on fire, while British Army vehicles roared about the place. I suppose it was exciting for a twelve-year-old country boy, but my aunt and uncle were distracted the following day when I went wandering down the Falls Road without telling anyone. Fascinated by barricades at every street corner, cars burned out and trees chopped down, I didn't return for about three hours. It had been a wee boy's dream. Needless to say, I was despatched back to the safety and quiet of Enniskillen as quickly as possible.

My dad's sister also married a Roman Catholic and I remember vividly two cousins coming to visit us in Fermanagh when I was around 12. My mother had arranged for us to take tea in the garden and on a beautiful sunny day, my cousins duly arrived. One had brought her new husband with her and he was black, the other was a nun in full regalia. I felt as if it was the worst day of my life. This was different in a big way and I would have loved to have gone indoors away from prying eyes. My mother had other ideas and insisted that the garden party continued for all to see.

I attended Portora Royal School, then an all-Protestant establishment that promised a good education, and discovered like my mother's people that I had a love for and an ability to make music. I took up the tuba and became a regular with the Western Counties Youth Orchestra and the Murley Brass Band from Fivemiletown in neighbouring Co Tyrone. I also occasionally played with St Colman's Brass Band from Strabane. Most of my friends in music were Catholics, including the actor Adrian Dunbar, although it never seemed to matter to me what anyone was. I was never bigoted, thank God, given the family and friends that I had, and I had many happy times playing on both sides of the border. Believe it or not, I continued to play at many of the same cross-border venues even after I had joined the Royal Ulster Constabulary.

It was the same with sport. As a member of Enniskillen Rugby Club, I played a lot of Sunday matches on the other side of the border at a time when that was unthinkable in the North. That continued for a number of years even after I joined the police and I remember it as great craic with lots of beer and traditional Irish music in the local pubs.

I passed out of the RUC's Enniskillen Training Centre as a constable at the age of 19, fresh out of school and with my ambition fulfilled. I loved the police, Enniskillen is a real police town, and felt as if I was doing my bit to improve things in this country. I made many friends and had good times, but there were many downsides, terrible downsides. I lost touch with my Catholic cousins, while most of the rest of my family remained close despite the conflict. The RUC was on one side, the Gaelic Athletic Association - to which many of my mother's family belonged and of which my uncle was the County Chairman - was on the other. There could be no common ground and the GAA even had a rule that forbade members of the force from playing Gaelic games. That's been rescinded in recent years and the Police Service of Northern Ireland now has its own Gaelic football team, but in those days the RUC and GAA were like sworn enemies.

I stayed firmly on my side of the fence and served in Fermanagh, Tyrone, Down - the city of Belfast - some of the same streets I had walked as an inquisitive twelve-year-old during more than 15 years in uniform. It's ironic that, by and large, I enjoyed my service given that my family and I know of around 70 RUC officers who were murdered during those terrible times. Tragedies that have scarred that part of the world.

I fell out of love with the police force after a colleague and I – off duty at the time – were assaulted by a crowd in East Belfast one Saturday evening. We were both badly shaken up, he suffered a broken leg and we were both disappointed that our superiors were less than sympathetic or supportive when we returned to duty. I felt let down and for me it was the last straw. It was 1990, a dark time, I felt that Northern Ireland had nothing more to offer me and that I had nothing more to give to it. I resigned, packed up, headed to Scotland, bought a small hotel in Ballantrae on the West Coast and I've been here ever since.

Thinking back, I used to consider myself British first, Irish second, but that has probably changed a wee bit over the years. My upbringing in rugby, golf, sport in general and music has helped me to see many things like these as Irish first. Rory McIlroy is another case in question I suppose. Most golfing people are glad that he chose to play for Ireland in the Olympics as they, like their rugby counterparts, regard their sports as Irish.

I have a real love of ballad singing and Irish songs in particular and try stopping me from singing when the drink is taken. When asked by some people if I'm Irish or British, I answer both! So I'm a wee bit like Sharon Stone – whatever takes her fancy at the time.

I still keep in touch with my family – of both persuasions – and try to get back to Fermanagh when I can, but my life is anchored in Scotland. I have made friends from back home, ironically on holiday in Spain, who are Republicans and we can banter about things. Times have changed for the better certainly, from bad old days of the 1970s and '80s, but I'm not overly optimistic about the political future of Northern Ireland.

I'm sorry to say that, but it's just that those in power seem to have too much to lose to make the extra step to compromise. They won't or can't lose face and there is little evidence that they even want to work together unselfishly for the future - if anything, it's the opposite.

Do I want a united Ireland? Not at all, and I don't think the people in the Irish Republic want Northern Ireland either. Having said that, the Republic is still my favourite country to visit. However, I do think of home often and hope for the best. I read the Belfast Telegraph online everyday to keep up with developments and the local Fermanagh newspaper, the 'Impartial Reporter' every week to see what's happening back in Enniskillen. That's where I read about NIMMA's book.

I hope that its young readers can learn something from these stories, something from my story. Even if it's just that mixed marriages aren't abnormal, that they're not about prejudice and bigotry, but rather love and compromise and that those two things should be celebrated.

David's mum and dad

The Case for Tolerance

Jenny is a 26-year-old Criminal Defence Lawyer based in Edinburgh. Ten years after she left Derry her Northern Ireland accent remains intact, her pride in her country intense, although she sees her professional future fixed firmly in Great Britain.

Life's full of contradictions and surely all the more colourful for that in my experience. I've been in Edinburgh since university days and after nearly ten years I can look back at Northern Ireland with fondness. I know that my home city of Derry has come on leaps and bounds and that there is now a great sense of hope for the future but, having said that, I know that I left home originally because of what I perceived as a lack of opportunity and for me nothing has changed on that front. I still see Northern Ireland as too small and lacking in professional opportunities and I can't see myself ever wanting to go back to live there, unless my family needed me desperately, but, having said that as well, I am very proud to come from there. A contradiction surely, but that's just the way it is. It will always be in my heart, but it will not be my home.

My mother, who is the youngest of four daughters, was born in Omagh in Co Tyrone to a middle-class Presbyterian family. Her father had served in the RAF and later worked for the Northern Ireland Civil Service. Her mother had been a clerical officer. The family moved to the leafy suburb of

Cherryvalley in East Belfast when mum was around eleven and all four girls attended the local grammar school. It was a church-going family, regularly attending Knock Presbyterian Church and committed to church activities including Sunday school. Ironic really as my grandfather later admitted that he had never been a believer, but thought it best for the family. Mum's was a sheltered existence, no Troubles, no Catholics, no bother. Until she went to study medicine at Queen's University.

Dad had been born and raised in Belfast. One of seven brothers from a devout Catholic family, he, like his siblings, served his time as an altar boy and went to the local Christian Brothers' Grammar school in the west of the city. There was absolutely no Republican agenda in the family but, given the geography of the place, he was certainly much more aware of what was going on than mum. That was the reality of living in what was termed the nationalist part of the city. He'd seen boys at school get 'involved' with paramilitaries, with all that that meant and I'm sure was glad that he had been raised in a family that cherished its faith, while respecting other people's beliefs. His decision to study medicine at Queen's was to prove a prescription for love and life.

Queen's was and still is a melting pot for young people from all over Northern Ireland, the vast majority of whom have been through an education system that has changed little since partition. My parents met, connected and started going out together. Nature has a way of subverting sectarianism. They had no problems while courting, no-one minding their business as it were, and their peers, a mixed bunch thought nothing of it. They were married in Knock Presbyterian Church in 1985 and, in keeping with tradition, in my mother's home church. Perhaps, not in keeping with the tradition of the time, everyone was happy about it. All invited attended, from both families, and, by all accounts, it was a great day. At first, Mum's father had had a fit about their relationship and even refused to speak to her for a while, but, decent man that he was, eventually wrote her a letter of apology and guided her down the aisle on the big day.

My parents moved to Derry when they qualified. Originally, mum was a bit scared of certain places in the city, given the reputation it had, her sheltered background and the fact it was the early 1980s, but they settled in the Waterside and started a family. My oldest sister Laura was born in 1986, I was next 1988, Jill came along in 1991 and perhaps religion was put into perspective. Jill was born with Down's syndrome. It was a massive shock for the family in the beginning, but one that they took in their stride. Brother Andrew was born in 1995. All four of us were baptised in the Catholic Church, incidentally by my father's uncle Fr Francis Coyle, but all of us attended Oakgrove Integrated Primary School. My parents were keen for us to be educated in integrated schools and got involved with Oakgrove at an early stage in its set up. It was the perfect accommodation for a mixed couple and, best of all, it meant that we could all go to the same school as Jill. Perfect. Mum has been on the Board of Governors of the school since the start, dad was also a governor of the College for a while.

I grew up with mainly Catholic friends, geography again dictating things. Derry was very Catholic, but my parents got round even that by sending us to Brownies, The Good News gospel club and dancing classes. All so we would have friends from both sides. It was a good idea and it worked. None of us made First Communion or Confirmation, probably just as well as we consider ourselves atheists now. I have no interest in the Christian faith, of whatever shade, and am still puzzled when I look back to the days when people at school 'identified' me in turn as a Catholic or a Protestant. It was probably a compliment that I should be able to pass for either at that time, but verbal abuse for both sounded just the same. Raucous and wrong-headed and another case of contradictions coming into complicate our lives. I'm just glad it was nothing more serious.

I had always wanted to be involved with the law, even from as young as 10 year old child. My father's late brother, who sadly passed away aged only 40, had been a criminal defence lawyer and I suppose I've had some inspiration from him. Amazingly, I remember his funeral and evidence of the law on show. Down one side of the church saw an array of his former clients - a right set of bruisers - while on the other side were his peers from the legal profession.

From early days at university in Edinburgh I also intended to be a criminal defence lawyer. I don't have a problem representing people for various crimes, but thought I'd always find terrorism difficult because of how it destroyed our country, so I thought it best to move to Scotland on a number of counts. If I had a son who wanted to be a policeman, I wouldn't want to live somewhere where his or his family's life would be in danger just because of his job. That's been the way in the Northern Ireland of the recent past, although I hope for a brighter, safer and more tolerant future.

Edinburgh proved a bit of a culture shock for me ten years ago. It's a 'posh' sort of a city – no too big as to swamp you as somewhere like London, but big enough and snooty enough to daunt a girl from a working class city like Derry. Notice I say Derry not Londonderry. Everyone back home calls it Derry, regardless of their religion. I took time to settle in Scotland, but now I've made friends, all of them Scottish with sound Labour affinities and no interest in religion, and consider it my home.

Somewhere along the line I've lost that special Northern Ireland curiosity about a person's religion. You know the one. Everybody back home has it, whether they admit or not. The sixth sense, the safety mechanism of a sort that people use to suss out someone's religion. They do it without even knowing. Most times not even out of prejudice, but rather about not wanting to offend another person. I've kept my accent, but I no longer think, care or even consider a person's religion. Scotland has done that for me and I'm grateful.

Scottish people are fiercely proud of their nationality and, as an exile, I've picked up on that sentiment. I'm proud to call myself Irish for all the right reasons and feel more patriotic than ever before, although it's got nothing to do with politics. People all over the world love the Irish and I like being part of that, but Edinburgh is now my home - although I have yet another St Brigid's cross on the back of my flat door courtesy of my father - and the law my career. I may be working on anything from drugs and traffic offences to murder, so I've got to be on top of my game. Regular visits to the gym and the odd half marathon certainly help and the support of friends is essential.

I know in my heart that things are improving back in Northern Ireland. I have confidence that our young people have moved on and have no time for that innate intolerance that blighted our country for so long. From my own direct experience, I see integrated education as a valuable resource in bringing people together and, like many others, I hope for its vast expansion in the future. However I feel it's a great shame and pity that the politicians, with the exception of the Alliance Party, show so little leadership, contradict each other at every turn and are so unrepresentative of a generation that wants to go forward. Their blind intolerance is indefensible.

The McCallion family

Respect and Love

Kit is a retired postal executive, originally from Portadown, who lives in Banbridge.
He acknowledges the example of respect and love learned from his parents.

I was born in 1955 in Portadown, seven years after my Catholic father and Presbyterian mother married. They had six children and we were raised Catholic. My two eldest siblings were regarded by the church as illegitimate as my parents had married in a Presbyterian Church and my father refused to conform to the demands of Ne Temere, the Catholic Church's rules on mixed marriages. For this he was effectively excommunicated and unable to receive the sacraments and as a devout practising Catholic this upset my father tremendously, an upset that would return to him during the last months of his life. He died in 2013, at 87 years of age, suffering from dementia.

My mother, also now in her 80s and still living, converted to Catholicism six years into the marriage when she was pregnant with me and they remarried in the Catholic Church. While the first two born, my eldest brother and sister, were regarded as 'illegitimate', the third, another older brother, was recognised as 'legitimate' because he was born while my mother was 'taking instruction' to convert. I was the fourth born, but the first to be born wholly within my parents' marriage as recognised by the Catholic Church. I know my mother was disappointed when I ceased attending Mass during my teenage years. Ironically, while my mother was attending classes to 'take instruction', my three older siblings were left to be minded by a Protestant neighbour whose husband was an Orangeman. They were to become life-long friends of my family.

When my eldest brother was born, my parents wished him to be baptised in the Catholic Church. However, this wasn't successful until he was 5 months old, as the Parish Priest refused to acknowledge my parents' marriage and frustrated them in an attempt to have their marriage conform to the Ne Temere decree. That was in 1949.

My parents met when my mother was 14 years old and my father 16 and they remained together for the next 70 years. When my father reached his 18th birthday in 1943, he joined the RAF for the war effort and was stationed in England and then Nutt's Corner near Belfast. My parents' wedding photo shows him wearing his RAF uniform outside Tandragee Presbyterian Church where they first married. If there are photos of their remarriage in the Catholic Church, I have never seen them and, as far as they were concerned, their wedding anniversary was the day they married not the day they remarried.

Their wedding was planned for 11 a.m. on Easter Tuesday 1948 while my father was on home leave from the RAF. His parents were vehemently opposed to the wedding and put pressure on him to cancel it, so he walked out of his home on Easter Monday and made his way to my mother's house. His parents followed him and continued to beg him not to marry my Protestant mother, which seems bizarre given that his father's father had been a Protestant. So secretly, my parents arranged for the wedding time to be brought forward from 11 a.m. to 8 a.m. the next morning and only the two witnesses plus a girl friend of my mother's and the minister were present. My mother recalls that it was raining heavily, but that they were both happy. They didn't receive any presents from my father's family until they remarried in the Catholic Church six years later.

Like most children, we were closer to my mother's parents and family than to my father's, even though my father's family lived locally and my mother's were in Bangor and Armagh. My father's mother died before I was born and his father died when I was eight years old, so I didn't know them. We had 12 Catholic first cousins in Portadown and one Protestant first cousin in Armagh who we felt closer to because our mothers were sisters. My mother and her older sister were my grandparents' only children. They had been born on the Shore Road in Belfast and had been child evacuees to Tandragee from the Belfast blitz in 1941. Growing up I remember there seemed to be a certain distance between us and our extended Catholic family. They were kind and friendly, but we were never really close. I was aware from an early age, probably around the time of my paternal grandfather's passing, that my father's two sisters and sister-in-law, my Catholic aunts, had not approved of his choice of wife, or rather her denomination. Although this was not manifested openly, I was always aware of a subtle discomforting undercurrent that they disliked my mother. Indeed, my mother only recently told me that when my teenage father declared to his mother that they were seeing each other, his mother responded by saying he would get nowhere going out with 'that wee Protestant girl'.

By contrast, my mother's mother, a church-going Presbyterian, would occasionally take the train from Bangor for weekend visits to Portadown when we were young children and she would attend Sunday Mass with us - her philosophy being that it didn't matter where you worshipped your God. We regularly travelled to Bangor on Sunday outings and summer breaks to stay with my grandparents who lavished us with much love and attention. As I grew older I realised that my grandfather would have described himself as agnostic at least and possibly even an atheist. I adored him. He worked for Belfast Corporation, what is now Belfast City Council, and was the only 'Protestant' in the Falls Road bus depot. He was the manager. In his later years he would recall to me many stories of his life, mostly about his service in India with the Royal Inniskilling Fusiliers in the 1920s, driving trams up the Limestone Road in the snow and about his wartime civilian medal, awarded for driving his bus through the bombings of the Belfast Blitz, taking many casualties to hospital. He took pride in telling me that his best friends were Catholic work colleagues from the Falls Road.

In Bangor we experienced the strong Scottish flavour of my mother's heritage. My grandfather bought the Scottish Sunday papers, the Sunday Mail and the Sunday Post, that exposed us to the cartoons of Oor Wullie and The Broons.

He loved music - and The Alexander Brothers and Andy Stewart records were commonly played. I particularly loved 'The Muckin' of Geordie's Byre'. He was a liberal man with working-class roots who didn't warm to the unionist government or the Orange Order and if he was alive today I think I would know his views on the Ulster Scots movement that has been largely politicised. Born in Belfast in 1899, with roots through County Monaghan to Ayrshire, he would have called himself Scots Irish, which he was to his toenails. And he didn't take to religion. Visiting Bangor once in early adulthood, my grandmother complained to me that a few Sundays earlier she had been unable to attend church because she was feeling poorly. Her minister decided to visit her later that week to see if she was well, but when my grandfather saw him walking up the path he sat on my grandmother so she couldn't answer the door.

When my parents married, my grandfather gave his daughter some advice, not to give the children Catholic names because, as he said, they wouldn't get a job. So we all have somewhat 'neutral' names. Given that my father's grandfather had been a Protestant and we inherited his English surname it was great fun growing up when people assumed we were Protestants and confided a political or religious opinion that would be disrespectful to Catholics. Depending on the circumstances, I would drop a few hints about my background and enjoy watching them wince and wither. In recent times, I was in my next door neighbour's kitchen when a salesman knocked on their front door and introduced himself as Kieran. My neighbour, an avowedly staunch unionist, politely declined Kieran's services and returned to the kitchen whereupon he declared to me, "We don't buy anything from Catholics". When my neighbours were moving house a few months later and we were chatting over the garden fence before they left, they raised the prospect of attending a different church, so I casually, and opportunistically, let it drop about going to Mass as a child. It was a real conversation stopper. Even though I had long since regarded myself as a non-Catholic and my neighbours were absolutely brilliant in every other sense, I found it really hard to resist subtly making them aware of their presumptuous faux pas.

I attended a convent primary school so was conscious of religion at an early age, although I can't remember when I became aware of the religious divide. Our class was taught by a lay teacher, Mrs McCann, a horrible, blue-rinsed woman who didn't like me. However, I don't think it was a religious thing, she was probably just a naturally unpleasant lady. I can vividly remember a nun giving our class a religious instruction lesson telling us about our Guardian Angels and how they would always look over us and protect us from evil so that we wouldn't go to Hell. She added that only Catholics had Guardian Angels, but that Protestants didn't believe in them and that they would go to Hell. I remember being upset that my granny wouldn't be going to heaven. I left that school when I was eight, so I was probably only six years old at the time. I must have been aware of religious differences at that point, although innocently so.

We lived in a religiously mixed housing estate, although predominantly Protestant. All my childhood friends were

Protestants and I collected for the local bonfire on the 11th night. One of my friends taught me to play 'The Sash' on the snare drum and I can still play it today. It was the happy 1960s. However, not all our neighbours were tolerant. My mother and I were walking home one afternoon and we were close to our house. She had me by the hand, so I must have been quite small. A woman who lived down the street from us and about my mother's age came towards us and let loose on my mother about how she was a 'fucking Fenian turncoat' shouting at the top of her voice in broad daylight in the street. She just tore into Mum with such violent verbal hatred. We got away and into the house and strangely I understood what the fuss had been all about. I knew what the contentious issue was even at that small age.

Many years later when my eldest brother, Jeff, was going through a divorce, he came to stay with me for a short while as I lived alone and had spare rooms. He was 50 years old and I would have been 44. We drank a lot. One night he told me a story he had never told anyone before, not even his now estranged wife during 30 years of marriage, who coincidentally was a Protestant. It was about an incident when he was nine years old and my older sister had been taking part in a school event at a local Catholic parish hall. She would have been seven. My mother had sent him to meet her coming out at the end of the event and bring her the short distance home. Arriving at the parish hall, Jeff was confronted by four women, around our parents' age, who were obviously there to meet their own children. On seeing him approach, one of the women declared loudly "Here's Vincie Wright's wee bastard", in reference to my father and the circumstances of Jeff's birth. Of course Jeff didn't understand this. They grabbed him and shoved him from one to another laughing and mocking him, while repeatedly calling him "Vincie Wright's wee bastard" until the parish hall doors opened. Jeff had lived all his adult life in England and kept that incident locked away for 41 years. He could still recall the women's names when he told the story for the first time, sitting on my settee drunk, with tears streaming down his face. It had affected him deeply for all those years and I wonder if a child psychologist would have attributed Jeff's lifelong stammer to that incident.

Thankfully the two incidents related to above were isolated and I firmly believe from life's experience that the misguided individuals involved are representative of only a tiny minority of intolerant people on both sides of the religious divide.

During the 1974 loyalist strike our house was petrol bombed and we were forced to move to a new housing estate on Portadown's Garvaghy Road which was gradually becoming a Catholic area due to increasing intimidation on both sides at that time. I never liked it there, as I always preferred mixed cultural company which was restricted due to the tensions of the time and the risk from a minority of bigots. Portadown became a polarised town during the 1970s and largely remains so today, although on the rare occasion I bump into one of my Protestant childhood friends or neighbours we share happy memories. I left the Garvaghy Road after five years to get married and my parents moved 25 years later to a new-build bungalow in a middle-class area. My mother said that she had finally come home as she had never chosen to move from our first house, but had been forced to. This time she chose.

My father had a difficulty with the institutions of the Catholic Church. He was devout in his faith, but had little tolerance of the politics of the Church. He regarded himself very much as an Irishman, even though having served in the British armed forces he would have been a 'soft' nationalist, but he despised Irish Republicans who used their Catholic faith as some kind of credential for their political beliefs. He would often tell me "The problem with Irish Catholics is that they are Irish first and they are Catholics second". For him his faith came first. It was what defined him and it came before any notion of national identity. He just happened to be born in Ireland.

When his RAF service ended my father went to the British Legion hall in Portadown to socialise, but hard-line unionists in the hall made him unwelcome because he was a Catholic. He never returned and refused to buy a poppy all his life because, while blaming the bigots for turning him away, he also took umbrage that the British Legion officers hadn't stood up to them on behalf of an ex-serviceman like himself. My mother would have liked to have worn the poppy in memory of her great uncle Jack Flanagan who fought in the Boer War and was a Recruiting Sergeant during the First World War, even though he didn't see battle. My mother was fond of him as he had married her mother's favourite aunt Ellen. Jack and my great, great aunt Ellen were the grandparents of a high ranking RUC officer during the 1990s. This was only one dimension of the strong RUC tradition on my mother's side.

This family connection ruefully came back to me when I attended a wedding on the extended Catholic side of my family in the early 2000s. My relative was the bride and was marrying a local Catholic man whose sister was married to a leading Republican with a high profile in the Drumcree Orange parade dispute. I spotted the Republican in the corner of the reception room, my relative now his sister in-law, and I remember thinking that I was now loosely related by marriage to one of the main protagonists on one side of the dispute and distantly related to one of the chief law enforcers on the other. We do live in a small village.

Many of my mother's uncles and first cousins were in the RUC. My own cousin also served for a few years and her husband was a career policemen. My cousin, who was some 8 years older than me, had me convinced at 14 years of age that I was joining the RUC when I left school. I would have been happy to, but The Troubles started and it didn't happen. However, the family connection gave me a degree of empathy for police officers that would not have been appreciated by some of my Christian Brothers' classmates in Armagh. Not that I was stupid enough to tell them, given the number that hailed from South Armagh. Three of my schoolmates were later killed 'on active service' in the IRA.

My brother, Bobby, who was two years older than me and attended the same Christian Brothers' school, had no such qualms. At 16 years old he decided to join the Royal Navy. He declared this during a careers' advice session and his careers' teacher, a Christian Brother, secretly arranged for a Royal Navy recruiting agent to visit Bobby at school to give him some advice. He joined up for four years before marrying and settling in Scotland, joining the Fife Constabulary and serving almost 30 years with them. We both played Gaelic football for Tir na Nog, the local club, and when Bobby came home on his first stint of Navy leave in 1970 he offered to join me for the regular Thursday night training session at the club grounds, called "The Hill". When we arrived, we were met at the changing room door by our trainer, a primary school teacher, who said it would be all right for me to take training, but as Bobby was now in the British forces he was no longer welcome. We returned home and I left the club voluntarily some months later. The following year when he was again home on leave and we were walking home from Portadown town centre on a Saturday afternoon, three boys who had been in Bobby's class at school ran across the road to confront us. They told him that he "should be shot" for joining the Brits. Bobby didn't return to Portadown for many years, even after leaving the Navy, as it was too dangerous for him. On the occasions when his two children were born, he visited my parents from Scotland staying a few days with me in Lisburn where I married, and it was a quick trip in and out of Portadown before anyone noticed.

I didn't think my mother's role as a Girl Guide Leader in her youth would be useful to me but she was able to offer some subtle advice to me in later years. I started working for the Post Office in the 1970s and at one point my duties included raising the Union flag over the local Post Office building on the days designated by government. Given my upbringing I didn't have a problem with this, but when I told my mother she was careful to explain to me the right way to raise it, not upside down. She was worried that as a Catholic I might take some criticism for doing this deliberately, even if I had done so accidentally. Another piece of advice was when I started playing in a rock band as a guitarist and lead singer. Knowing the prevailing custom of playing the national anthems in pubs and dancehalls, depending on which side of the divide you were entertaining, she was able to explain which lines went "God save the Queen" and "God save our Queen", avoiding any potential for getting a kicking in some drunken back street club.

My younger sister was widowed in her early thirties when the UVF murdered her husband, who was a taxi driver and randomly targeted. They had two pre-school aged children. My Protestant aunt, her husband and my cousin did not attend his funeral and a remark on my brother-in-law's killing was passed that 'there was no smoke without fire'. They hadn't attended my sister's wedding 5 years earlier either as my aunt's husband was an Orangeman. My sister refused to talk to them for many years until my aunt's husband apologised to her after both his wife and daughter had pre-deceased him.

My sister later married again to a Protestant, a great guy who I am lucky to have as a brother-in-law. He didn't think twice about taking on her two children. They had a civil ceremony in a Registry Office and had a son of their own in 1996, at the beginning of the 'Peace Process'. After some careful consideration they decided to have their son baptised into the Catholic Church like his two older half siblings. However, they were frustrated in doing so by the local Parish Canon who refused to acknowledge the legitimacy of their marriage. He relented when my sister walked out of their discussion bluntly telling him she would baptise her son in another denomination. In 1949 my parents were similarly frustrated in having my eldest brother baptised, it seemed nothing had changed in 47 years.

One unexpected aspect of being the child of a mixed marriage was medical history. When I was diagnosed with cancer on the eve of my 52nd birthday and then my brother received the same bad news a few years later, my GP advised me to speak to the cancer genetics department at Belfast City Hospital to determine if there was a trend in the family history. If a trend was found this would enable us to alert the next generations of the family and they would be aware of the need for early checks. However, as my parents had largely been distanced from their immediate and extended families, we didn't have any information on how relatives of previous generations had died. I did eventually source the information through a cousin of my mother who lived in Canada and who had remained sympathetic and loyal to my mother through all the years.

My father developed dementia in his early eighties, although we now recognise earlier signs. His gradual descent into the dark recesses of his mind was painful to watch. When our eldest, Jeff, died suddenly of a heart attack, Dad cried for a moment then forgot. We had to hide the Irish News that listed Jeff's death notice because he would read it and cry, then forget he had read it. He would then read it again and cry again. Jeff was an atheist and wanted a Humanist funeral service which was held in a funeral home in Bangor. It was an operation to get my father there, but we couldn't tell him it was his son's funeral because he would have been upset that there were no priests present, forgetting that Jeff had long since given up his Catholicism.

Dementia gradually erodes the memory and over three years Dad's memory rewound from the most recent times when he was a driving instructor, to postman, then bus driver, RAF service and finally schoolchild. My mother watched this and it brought recognisable memories back to her. In the last month of his life he became extremely frail. He must have known he was dying because he prayed so feverishly. His withered, shaking hands clasped together as he whispered unrecognisable words of prayer with what seemed to us some urgency. He would try to bless himself, but physically couldn't, so my sister would lift his right hand and make the gesture for him. My mother recognised that he was trapped in a belief that he was still excommunicated, but could not remember being allowed back into the Church. He was praying to stay out of Hell. At 57 years of age, I and my surviving siblings were still witnessing the torment that was created because of his love for my mother.

Overall my parents had a happy life and they raised us to be respectful and discreet. When we were old enough to look after ourselves they took off around the world on exotic holidays in Europe, the USA, Canada and Australia. Their humble working class origins inspired aspirations to better themselves and improve the prospects for their children and we all went on to attain higher educational achievements and pursue more professional careers. Of the six children my parents gave life to, three married Protestants, one a Buddhist, one a Catholic (who ironically later divorced) and the other never married. We too experienced an overall happy life. However, standing at my Dad's bedside during the last days of his life and witnessing the torment that was instilled in him some 70 years earlier, it brought me back to my early memories of the family discomfort that I had long since forgotten. Dementia had erased almost a lifetime of his memory, but it couldn't impact upon the deepest wound on his psyche, the torture he had to endure for loving my mother.

I often wondered throughout the years of the 'Troubles' why high profile people of influence in politics and the churches could only highlight differences between us when it was obvious to me that there were none. These negative and damaging influences were manifested in the worst of my experiences with my extended family on both sides, but these were small in comparison to the good experiences. It deeply disappoints me that these sectarian, malignant voices are still as loud today and try to be as influential as before when the fact is that the high level of tolerance, respect and love that survived the 'Troubles' still sustains us. Those voices have a lot to learn from people like my parents.

Kit's mum and dad

Pretty Normal

Ben Clarke is an 'A' Level student at Regent House School, Newtownards. He is a remarkably mature young man who has his sights set on a university education in the United States. He sees his long-term future in the USA, rather than in Northern Ireland.

I won't be seventeen until November 2014, so I'm not sure how much I have to say about being the child of a mixed marriage, other than it feels pretty normal to me. Maybe that's important in itself. My Aunt Mary, who's a journalist, thought I would make a good candidate for this book, probably for just that reason, but it's not something that I've given a lot of thought to be honest.

Some of my friends were shocked to learn that my parents come from different denominations – the Protestant and Catholic thing – and I was surprised at that. Maybe mixed marriage is something that's not talked about or maybe not talked about enough. I didn't talk about it, didn't even consider it really and now, well, it's not something that worries me.

There will always be jokes and banter about religion in this country. Some jokes with jags sadly, but maybe in the long run that's healthy.

As far as I'm concerned I'm just a normal post GCSE student who happens to be the child of a mixed marriage. I admit to being a typical teenager in many ways, although I am planning for the future a bit more than most people of my age - I have to. The things I want in the years ahead are just that little bit more complicated.

I have two years real graft in front of me for four 'A' levels, while preparing for tests and interviews for a university place in the United States. It's something I want to do and, hopefully, all the hard work that lies ahead will be worth it in the end. Meantime, like I say, I'm normal. I love football, playing five-a-side with my mates and supporting Manchester City in the Premier League. That support goes back long before they became successful. I also enjoy writing about football and I've been writing pieces for an online blog that specialises in the top tier of the English game.

I live in Bangor and the 'mixed' thing doesn't really come into it. I don't really know or care what religion or denomination my friends or neighbours are. That's not important. I was baptised a Catholic and still go to Mass occasionally with my mother and grandmother, but God is a difficult one for me at the moment and I don't really know what to believe or even to believe at all. I think that's pretty normal for a guy of my age.

Although subtle, I believe that my parents' mixed marriage has had an impact on me. They come from totally different backgrounds. My Mum had quite a devout Catholic upbringing and still attends Mass regularly, although my

Dad, while Protestant, is not religious in a church-going sense. All the same my folks seem to have struck a good balance in their relationship, despite those differences and I suppose that my being comfortable with the whole mixed marriage thing is testament to their efforts. I guess that my indifference to the religious divide in this country is due to my upbringing. My parents come from either side of a metaphorical barrier, but they love each other just the same - why can't everyone in this country follow this example?

My parents, who both came from Belfast's Lisburn Road district, met through mutual friends and just carried on from there. I know that they had their share of problems back then. They met with a certain amount of opposition from both families during their courtship, with both sides hoping that it wouldn't result in marriage and my Catholic Granny used to say that 'families that don't pray together, don't stay together'.

Some of my Dad's so-called friends even refused to attend the wedding stating that as members of the Orange Order they would not be allowed to attend, but others, who were also members, did. Sadly, there are always stupid people. I know now that my parents made a very conscious decision to move out of Belfast to have some kind of 'anonymity'. To me that decision was both brave and appropriate.

Personally I don't have any horror stories about school, the opposite in fact. I attended a state-controlled primary at Kilmaine just down the road and a funny story comes to mind of a boy from my class asking if I was a cat or a dog. I was eight years old, I said I was a cat and he sort of automatically said, "Oh you're a Catholic then". We laughed and that was that. Daft and that's probably as good an advert for integrated education as early as possible.

I'm really a Catholic in name only anyway. I didn't make First Communion or Confirmation and, although if I was pushed I would probably identify more with the Catholic faith than any other, I think that's just because it's all I've ever experienced fully.

In saying that, I'm just back from a Christian summer camp where I went with friends. I enjoyed getting away and the craic, but the whole Christian thing went over my head I'm afraid. Maybe it's because I see religion as a negative thing. It looks that way in Northern Ireland terms. I see people dwelling in the past and using religion like a stick to beat the other guys. I just don't see the point of being involved with something so divisive.

I hate bigotry and prejudice of any kind and I'm very glad I've experienced so little of it myself. I've listened to Protestant schoolmates at grammar school talk about how 'Catholics worship the Pope' and think that it's sad that such nonsense is passed down from generation to generation here, creating a seemingly endless cycle of bigotry.

There is a boy at school who's Catholic, very Irish and quite outspoken who gets a bit of stick from the lads on the bus. They sing the Sash and that kind of thing, but he is well able for it and probably enjoys the attention. However, every once in a while he goes quiet and I can see how deeply the consistent teasing cuts him. I just think it's stupid to base treatment of someone on their background, no matter where they're from. He's a great, funny guy, but within my school he'll always be known as 'That Catholic'.

I regard all that Protestant/Catholic, Irish/British stuff as a waste of time. I'm Northern Irish because I come from Northern Ireland and British I suppose, but I look forward to having not much to do with any of it. Politics and identity go hand in hand in this country, divisions here are so deep and opinions so opposite that any form of compromise looks impossible. Even if there was a will, I don't think there is a way. I know little about discrimination or trouble and want no part of either.

I don't see my future in Northern Ireland at all. My sights are set on university in the United States and a life there afterwards. I will have to work like a dog to achieve that, but what's a few years sacrificed compared to the 50 or so I'll have after that. I've been on holiday to California and it was the best. I'm not naive enough to think that university will be some sort of holiday, but it will be the experience of a lifetime and will give me a real feel for the place and its people before I possibly take up a career in business there.

I'm hoping to go with my friend Kai, and we're looking to GO somewhere, not just to GET AWAY from Northern Ireland. I will miss my parents certainly – I have so much to thank them for in so many ways – but I won't miss certain parts of Northern Ireland. Sure, I'll miss many of the people, and I'll miss Bangor itself, but as for the reputation that comes with a residence in Northern Ireland, I'll be glad to see the back of it.

I'm extremely proud of my upbringing and in some deeper sense my country, but I just can't see myself spending the rest of my life here due to these pointless divisions and endless talk of bomb scares and sectarian violence. I wish it well for the future, for some kind of normality, but I hope it's from the other side of the Atlantic.

Ben's mum and dad

Do unto Others

Tinya from Lisburn enjoys a blend of two very different cultures, but turned to the East in her quest for inner peace.
Religion, and how it is defined in Northern Ireland, I find intriguing, but, personally, means very little to me. The whole Catholic/Protestant divide, the antagonism and territorial arguments seem less than Christian and, very much, leave me cold. I learnt tolerance and acceptance of others very early on: my moral compass coming ironically, from the most basic of Christian teachings - 'Do unto others as you would have them do to you'. Something my father deeply believed and taught me.

My father is English, from the beautiful Vale of Evesham – a world away from the Northern Ireland to which he came as a serving military policeman in the 1970s. He was brought up in the Church of England, but non-practising and verging on the agnostic. He was very different to the Belfast woman he would meet and marry.

My mother I romantically see as a sort of hippy in those days. She came from a liberal Catholic home, raised in the rather cosmopolitan surroundings of the city's Botanic Avenue. She drove a Mini with flowers painted on it, but this later got written off by a nearby IRA bomb. My grandfather, a civil servant was the example of tolerance – one of my three uncles even served in the RUC. My grandmother, not so tolerant, was concerned about the added danger my father might bring to the family. They say that love knows no boundaries and this unlikely pair – the military man and the free-spirited woman - proved that when they decided to marry.

When my father, who had agreed to be married in a Catholic church, refused to make the 'promise' that all children would be raised as Roman Catholics, my mother's parish priest told her that she would be excommunicated. My mother would have been happy to bring us up Catholic, she was quite a devout believer, but my father could not be hypocritical. He could not make a promise that he was in no position to keep. As a result, the wedding was held in one of those beautiful Evesham churches with a military guard. Not a million miles from Belfast, but it might as well have been. Nine months later I was born near that beautiful Evesham village.

Religion, however, did not play much of a role in my upbringing. Neither I, nor my only brother Scott, who is eight years younger than I am, were baptised and, as I've said, I care nothing for organised religion, looking in as a concerned observer. Mum took me to chapel occasionally, despite being excommunicated. I remember that annually being part of the magic of Christmas and Easter, but then so were the toys, Santa and chocolate eggs. I admit that I flirted with Christianity in primary school. Our home village of Moira was a very Christian sort of place and as a nine and ten year old I took up with friends who were 'born again'. I tried all of the churches in the village, probably wanting to fit into some group and out of a deep curiosity – the 'happy clappy' atmosphere of the evangelicals being quite appealing.

I remember the fun side of it, the social aspect and friendships, but I also recall the worry that I would somehow have to prevent my parents from going to hell by 'saving' them. It felt like a huge responsibility to put on myself, but that was what the church had me fear. Thankfully, secondary school, the onset of my teens and a lot of rational thinking put all that behind me. I felt happier for it.

'The Troubles' brought their own brand of stress and strain to thousands of people in this country as well as my family. My father had left the forces and become a prison officer. He served in the Maze Prison during some of its worst times and his job brought with it the kind of pressures and threat that only the blackest of humour could deal with.

There were the daily sweeps of the family car, constant vigilance against the threat of booby trap bombs. Long-handled mirrors, special three-light gadgets, fitted to the dashboard, were there to help you feel you had some control of your safety. But these devices malfunctioned from time to time or were set off by simple things like shopping trollies. I still remember one occasion when the lights signalled a possible bomb – but my Dad, knowing it was a false alarm, turned on the ignition and shouted 'Boom'. Humour doesn't come any blacker, but like many of his comrades it was their coping mechanism and we all learned to cope.

Unfortunately stresses also took their toll on many marriages and my parents separated when I was 15. Religion didn't play a part in the split, but Mum returned to the church and it has been a comfort to her during times of ill health.

Growing up I was confident about my identity. I was British, but not politically. I loved my English heritage, but was passionate about my home in Northern Ireland. However, a work transfer to West Belfast was to change how I saw Northern Ireland. I started work in the Suffolk and Andersonstown area in 1999, a Republican heartland, where being Irish seemed to be everything. My Dad was worried that I would be in danger, my mother concerned that somehow, as someone deemed to be a Protestant, I would suffer discrimination or be ostracised by staff and customers. That couldn't have been further from the truth.

I was welcomed, befriended and got my first taste of Irish culture first-hand. Words and language I had never even heard before became commonplace and myths and murals, a strange backdrop, became increasingly familiar over the years. These times changed my attitudes and gave me an insight into a culture in which, surprisingly at first, I felt I wanted more of a share.

As a child, the Republic of Ireland had been off-limits to our family. It wasn't really mentioned. It would probably have been unsafe. We had holidays with family in England. I had had the odd trip to Dublin with Co-operation North and even met the former President, Mary Robinson, but I don't think I realised the significance of it at the time or appreciated the relationship building that was going on. As an adult, I was free to experience new things and new places. I was curious about it and keen to take a look.

Unlike me, my husband Paul, who had a very Protestant upbringing, had explored the length and breadth of Ireland with his family and loved it. With an ageing motorhome he showed me the places he had been taken to as a child. I loved it, enjoying the relaxed attitude of its people, their idiosyncrasies and the warmth of their welcome. We camped and walked and photographed our way through Ireland, but especially Donegal, the northernmost county that is ironically in 'The South'. It was and remains one of my favourite places and has a very special place in my heart.

My grandfather's people are from the Glens of Antrim and I suspect that something in my roots has helped endear me to the wild places and welcoming folk of Ulster's North West. As it is, I feel now that I have a bit of both cultures living happily within me and I feel all the better for that. Northern Ireland, the political deadlock, the uncertainty about the future and the sheer waste of good people can be depressing in the extreme. Paul and I tried unsuccessfully to emigrate to Canada some years back and were disappointed to be refused on a technicality, but maybe it was for the best. We came to terms with it and have made our life here in a country that should be proud of its diversity, not fighting over it.

My brother also had the travelling bug, and, as well as seeing the world, he moved to Portugal to study for a PhD. Maybe given our background, it shouldn't be so unusual that it should have been his travels abroad – even to Tibet and the home of the Dalai Lama that sparked my interest in non-Christian spiritualism. I'm happy to say that my spiritual perspectives now have widened to include some 'God 'centred Buddhist teachings with their mindfulness, serenity and personal search for inner peace that doesn't rely on a God.

I am happy to have roots in both traditions, but belong to neither religion. When asked, which is rare nowadays, what religion I am or I come from – I openly say 'Both and neither'. My hopes for the future centre on a Northern Ireland where respect is more important than any religion or flag. I can't honestly think of a more honest and harmonious roadmap for the years ahead and I'm sure that example of mixed marriages will contribute to this.

Tinya's mum and dad

Many Gifts

Grace is an 18-year-old student from Banbridge, who is studying medicine at Queen's University Belfast. Her outstanding 'A' level performance this year is matched only by her natural modesty.

I have had only positive experiences as the child of a mixed marriage. Is that unusual? I don't think so. I see the love that my parents have for each other in action every day and how they work together to make our lives better. It is the best of examples and I know that they are doing their best to bring us up to show respect and tolerance to all regardless of denomination. I think it's the right way and this book has given me the chance to share that with others. I think it can help.

My parents come from totally different backgrounds and would probably never even have met if they both hadn't gone to work for Royal Mail. My mum is from West Belfast's Falls Road, my dad from Banbridge. She is a devout Catholic, he is a non-practising member of the Church of Ireland. They knew each other for more than a year before going out together and I think that 'friendship first' was a good thing. Mum feels that making a mixed marriage brought her closer to her faith. She is a Eucharistic Minister at our local church and considers that a real blessing. I can understand that totally. I was an altar server when I was younger and regard that as a privilege.

Mum and Dad were lucky when they met. In the 1980s, Royal Mail employed hundreds of young people from right across the religious spectrum and it was a melting pot that produced and encouraged mixed relationships. My parents were married in Belfast, chose to live in Banbridge and my two brothers and younger sister and I were raised Catholic. However, we didn't go to Catholic schools. My parents decided that Bridge Integrated Primary School would be best. They are both strong advocates of integrated education, believe that it enriches children from an early age and are of the opinion that religious education is best carried out in the home with support from chaplains at school.

I was in Primary Four before I even realised that I was a Catholic and that was only because First Communion was coming up. I never felt any different from any of my friends, either before or after. I can honestly say that religion was never an issue in those early years when we made friends because we liked one another, not because of some religious clique.

Eventually, I went on to Banbridge Academy, which is a grammar school with a majority of Protestant pupils, but I have never experienced anything even remotely sectarian or anti-Catholic in all my seven years there. In fact, when two other girls and myself completed our Pope John Paul II awards, our head master was invited to come to the awards ceremony in the chapel on a Sunday. Not only did he come, but he also brought seven of our teachers as well and then sent us letters saying how proud he was of us for our work in our church community. I thought that was lovely and very welcoming of the school.

Of course, there's been a bit of banter and even the odd joke about Catholics in general, but nothing malicious and definitely nothing directed at me as a person. Interestingly, we spent the first three years of religious education at the Academy learning about other faiths entirely and it wasn't until fourth year that we actually started reading about Christianity. Even then, it was mainly about Christian ethics and how to live your life in a respectful way. There is nothing divisive about that and I certainly didn't feel any different because of my denomination.

My friends are a mixed bunch as well, although I don't think about that at all. They are my friends first and foremost and their religious beliefs or lack of just don't come into it. I took up Irish Dancing three years ago and one friend of mine, who is a Protestant, joins me for the class, enjoys it every week before heading for flute band practice immediately afterwards. She's certainly seeing both sides of the culture on offer. And why not?

I find it easy to empathise with both 'sides' of my own family. I love my grandparents for who they are, not what they are, and I have seen nothing but respect and tolerance throughout my family and my home. I know I have been lucky and I hope to live my life in a similar way.

I think I have quite a logical mind – my parents might disagree with that – and I'm taking three sciences and maths for 'A' level. I hope I'm the type of person who thinks about things, rather than making rash decisions. I want to study medicine at Queen's University, like my older brother Mark, and hope to make my career as a

General Practitioner. I've worked as a volunteer in the admin side of a GP's surgery in Craigavon and know that this is right for me. Medicine is not for the squeamish and I've no qualms about what I will have to face in the future. I've done aptitude tests, interviews and even a role play session in which I had to pretend to be a doctor and now I await the results of the selection process with a lot of hope and not a little trepidation.

We are fortunate to have good community relations in Banbridge and my experiences as a member of the Banbridge Youth Bank, an organisation that raises and distributes money for community ventures, has given me an insight into how our 'whole' community – not sides, not factions and not different denominations - can and should work. The Youth Bank has given me quite a lot of responsibility in the past couple of years on things such as the Community Garden for the town, but it is also a lot of fun and you have to have fun when you're 18. Don't you? Fun certainly doesn't include politics however. I have absolutely no interest in party politics here. I don't dwell on things like nationality. I just don't think it's that important. I'm in the enviable position of feeling empathy with both sides of the Northern Ireland 'divide' and like to think that I can see the bigger picture. I suppose if I had to say one or the other, I'd say neither and go for Northern Irish. That's how I feel.

I've been to Corrymeela and seen the great work that starts there and spreads throughout our country. It's a fine example to all and makes me feel optimistic about the future. I have been brought up to show respect to others –

no matter who they are – and see that as one of the real advantages of being from a mixed background. I would like more availability of integrated education right across Northern Ireland and more Christianity taught by parents in the home.

I've watched the two people I love most in the world make a marriage of more than 25 years that is less about denominational differences and more about Christian love. I've seen my father take us to Mass when my Mum was away and seen the look of pride on his face as we made our First Communions and Confirmations. That is about love too. I am close to my family and university will be a wrench for sure and, although I don't know where my career and ambitions will take me in the years to come, I do know that wherever I go I will take with me the many gifts, like respect and tolerance, that have been handed down to me by my parents.

Grace's mum and dad

Where are you from?

Siobhan Mullin is a mother of two from Omagh. She has worked for the past eleven years as a care support worker in a residential and detox unit for alcoholics in the town. Siobhan fears for the future, but life has taught her to be determined and unafraid to face whatever it may bring.

I've always worked as a carer in some capacity. Looking back I'm sure that being the oldest of four children made me take responsibility for my brothers and sister from an early age and things just developed from there as I looked for a career. I have powerful memories of a particular time in my life and how I felt that I had to look after them. That must have sparked something in me and I eventually went to work with the elderly, people with learning disabilities and, since 2003, with those facing the horrors of alcoholism.

That has been an eye-opener if ever it was needed. To see how human beings, no matter their religion or social standing, can be brought so low by dependence can be frightening, but it is also humbling to see the success that our work has had and the positive impact it continues to have on so many fractured lives. There are people of most denominations and none that come through these doors in search of help and support and they are treated equally and with respect. A lesson to all of us I think.

Mixing seems to have had a special place in my family. My maternal grandmother was born in India – in the days of the Empire – and was half Portuguese and half English. She met my grandfather Reuben, a career soldier who had fought in the Boer War, while he was stationed in India and newly married they returned to the village of Drumquin in Co Tyrone when he retired from the army. A culture shock for them both I'm sure.

They had married in the Church of Ireland, although I've never been able to find out which denomination granny belonged to. It didn't seem to matter. They settled to rural life very well, she as a housewife, he as the local postman and their exotic days were behind them.

My late mother Maureen, who passed away two years ago, was born in 1947 and brought up in the Church of Ireland, although none of the family was gospel greedy and little would have changed had she not met my late father Tomas O'Reilly. Mum was already engaged to another fella when fate brought her and dad together. It was a love match from the start.

Dad was ten years older, had been born in Co Cork to a Tyrone family and had spent his youth travelling. He had been all over the United States and many more places besides and must have cut a foreign figure in a wee place like Drumquin. To cut a long story short, the two of them hit it off immediately, the engagement ring was returned and, within a fortnight, mum and dad had decided to marry. It was 1967 before the start of The Troubles, but at a time when Protestant and Roman Catholic existed, rather than lived, together. Country villages were just as divided along sectarian lines as the cities and word of the impending marriage set tongues wagging. Some said mum was pregnant and had to marry, some said worse and many acid-tongued nosey parkers seemed intent on minding my mother's and father's business.

They decided to get away from it all by moving to England, killing two birds with one stone – getting peace and work at the same time. They had two wedding ceremonies. I think there was a civil ceremony first of all that was followed by a blessing of some sort, but as neither of my parents was particularly religious I'm sure the blessing was for the benefit of grandparents and other family members. At that stage, dad's mum, Granny O'Reilly ran a pub in the village and was very well known.

I was born in 1968, by which time my parents were running their own pub in the London Borough of Norbury. Life was good, my brother and later another sister were born and I, the little girl with the South London accent, loved my primary school where I had many friends. No-one cared a jot about my Irish name or my perceived religion. I was among friends of all sorts. My memories of that time are warm and happy and have left me with a feeling that English people, though much maligned, are actually a lot more tolerant and welcoming than many people here give them credit for.

I had made my First Communion and our growing family was being raised Roman Catholic despite the fact that my mother was Protestant. She had even attended a special course designed to show 'non-Catholics', as they were described, how to raise children as 'good Catholics'. Like everything she did, she gave it her best shot and it's through no fault of hers that I am the lapsed Catholic that I am today. Far from it.

The year of 1978 proved a turning point for all of us. Mum had been heart-sore with homesickness for a very long time and, eventually, my parents decided to make a new life back in Northern Ireland. It seems crazy now with hindsight to swap the peace and normality of Norbury for a place that had seen nearly ten years of trouble, but it was what mum wanted and dad wanted mum to be happy.

Suddenly, we were back in Drumquin. It was a big change for all of us, but a massive one for me. I was nearly eleven years old, the eldest of three children and facing a world I knew absolutely nothing about. My younger brother and I would find out just how massive on our first day at our new school. From then on the 11 and 8 year old were constantly asked who they were, what they were, bullied for being Fenians in the state school, for being English in the Roman Catholic school that followed.

It was a traumatic time that I wouldn't wish on my worst enemy and it had a huge impact on me on me emotionally. I was big sister, but I became protector as I defended my brother and myself from verbal and physical abuse. It makes me angry and sad to remember the cruelty of children, but in a weird way it helped make me the person I am today. I still look to defend the underdog and I back down from nobody. I learned hard lessons being the child of a mixed marriage, being somehow different, about the ignorance of people toward children like me and about bullying and name calling.

Mum and dad settled back to village life. Dad even founded a boxing club to keep local kids off the streets. Our families rallied round us eventually. Things had been said, particularly on mum's side of the family, but blood's thicker than water and with the support of both families our lives got better. I'm glad to say that I have the love and friendship of both sides of my family, especially my Protestant and Catholic cousins who, from they were children, took us for what we were – their cousins.

For a while, I had felt so alienated that I thought it was me against the world. It was, but it has helped make me a stronger person. I always felt that I had to protect and I still feel that. I hate bullies and name callers of any kind and don't think about, let alone talk about, politics of any kind. In Northern Ireland politics divide people – it's that simple. My mum and dad never mentioned them and they got along just fine. I hate to think that sectarianism will continue to blight our country, but, if I'm honest, I see a divided future that simply won't change for many reasons. Prejudice, money, power, ignorance – take your pick.

I hope that the message of my story and the other stories in this book can do something to educate and improve the understanding of our young people, for them to realise that it's really okay to be different, it's okay to take people for themselves and not their religions or nationalities. I still feel British after all these years, people still say I have the strangest accent and I still get the odd 'where are you from?' I'm from my mum and dad – the Protestant and the Roman Catholic - and I'm proud of it.

A Better Future

Emma Thompson, 33, originally from Ballymena, works as a merchandiser for the international wing of a major retailer and lives in the London borough of Fulham. She has travelled extensively in the past ten years, but will return to live in Northern Ireland after her autumn wedding to fiancé Aidan.

Fate is such a mysterious thing when you come to think about it. Who we are, where we are born – the big questions in life – often depend so much on circumstances. I know from personal experience just how fate plays its part in those circumstances.

I am the child of a mixed marriage, with all that that entails, especially within Northern Ireland. I have travelled the world since leaving university, yet in only a matter of weeks, I'll be marrying my fiancée who I've known since schooldays. That might not sound like such a case of Kismet until I say that I hadn't seen him for years before bumping into him, almost literally, in a Sydney supermarket. Yes, 11,000 miles from home and Aidan and I met again, quite by chance, over the oranges and grapes in an Australian grocery store. Now that's fate and something I feel certain that was meant to happen. I see my parents' marriage as something similar. Fate brought Aidan and I together in the most unlikely of circumstances, just as it did Mum and Dad forty years before.

My father, who comes from a staunch Presbyterian background in the predominantly Protestant village of Garvagh in South Derry/Londonderry, was working as a bouncer at the time in a Portrush dance hall. Portrush was a Mecca for young people from all over the Province in those days and one evening the former amateur boxer, who fought proudly under the Tricolour for Ireland on a number of occasions, fell for the dark-haired young girl from Glenariff who was to become my mother.

They came from totally different backgrounds, yet even back then in the dark days of the 1970s it just didn't seem to matter. At least not to them and those they loved. They clicked, they courted, they fell in love – they still are by the way after 35 years of marriage – and they were wed in the wee chapel in Waterfoot, at the foot of one of the Glens, where I'll be married, with all their families, loved ones and friends gathered to support them. Oh, and the Roman Catholic priest doing the honours. I'm told it was a wonderful day and I know it was a shared beginning to a happily shared life together.

I've watched them for as long as I can remember and my greatest hope is that my future husband and I can enjoy as affectionate and demonstrative a relationship. Their love isn't soppy or sentimental, but unlike many couples of their generation, they are not afraid or embarrassed to show it. And I'm very proud of that.

Fate may have brought them together, the Protestant from the Plantation town and the Roman Catholic from the 'Queen of the Glens', but love has ensured that they have stayed together.

I was born two years later, baptised in that same little Waterfoot church and attended Catholic schools, including St Louis in Ballymena where I met Aidan. I made my first Holy Communion and Confirmation in turn and no-one was prouder on both days than my Dad. He has had his differences with the Roman Catholic Church on a number of issues over the years – haven't we all if we're being honest – but his respect for its people and their faith has never wavered.

I'm glad to say that such archaic vows as the 'all children Catholics promise' are now a thing of the past and good riddance and that all churches now recognise that the parents of children must be free to choose how they are reared. That seems like common sense to me and better still, common decency.

Perhaps, on reflection, my own upbringing might have been a little more 'mixed' than it actually was had fate not intervened as it did. My father, who is a joiner, and a good one at that, was compelled for economic reasons to travel abroad to work in places like France and Germany. My mother was left to do the bulk of the parenting at that time and she did her best to ensure that, despite my exclusively Catholic upbringing, I was well aware of both sides of the religious coin. It must have worked, because today I feel a little bit of both and all the happier for it.

I'm proud to be Irish certainly, yet hold a British passport and the reason is simple. When you've travelled as much as I have, the home country with the greatest number of consulates always seemed like the safest bet. Seriously though, I can relate to both cultures that are part of who I am and I would rather have what I have: an understanding and empathy for both.

In Northern Ireland, we can be so infuriatingly near-sighted and parochial. In Sydney, where I lived for three years, to be Irish was everything and everything that everyone wanted to be. It brought instant belonging, instant friends of all persuasions, an instant social circle and a real sense of community on the other side of the planet. It brought out all the good things about being from this part of the world and, amazingly, none of the bad.

One of our friends, an Orangeman from Ballyclare, who flexed his muscles to good effect on our Aussie Gaelic football team, was as Irish as anyone and certainly a better footballer than most. That's the kind of thing I would love to see happening in Northern Ireland. We have so much to offer each other and it's only a handshake away.

I'm not a particularly political person. Back in Fulham, I don't even vote, but I'd like to see local politicians in Northern Ireland pay more than lip service to the goal of a shared future. They have a responsibility to lead and they are not leading by example. I have my religious faith and my faith in Northern Ireland's future and the two things aren't mutually exclusive. We are all in this together and it is up to all of us to make the best of it.

I feel lucky in that I've had 'layered' upbringing, a chance to experience both sides of my past that I think gives me a broader, more liberal view of the world and I'm sure my travelling has helped lift the blinkers as well. Both my parents are churchgoers and I get a real kick out of accompanying my Dad to his service when I'm back home. Perhaps, it's just that I like being in his company.

Aidan and I are investing our future in Northern Ireland. We will be giving up our lives and careers in London and relocating to the Ballymena area after we get married, but even so, I am not overly optimistic about what lies ahead. The cynic in me says that too many people are holding power and making money from disagreement and division, but still I hold out hope. I've seen how my parents have coped and succeeded in their relationship and feel that our wider society has much to learn about how mixed marriage couples lead their lives.

People here are the best in the world – why else would we want to come back here – the quality of life, particularly for young children and families, is as good as it gets in these islands and it's time we caught ourselves on. When it comes to sectarianism, I say 'get over it', get a life and give others, especially our young folk the chance of a better future.

I'd like to finish with a word about my parents. Recently, Aidan and I went to a Roman Catholic marriage preparation course during which he was asked for an example of a good and loving marriage. The expected answer may well have been Mary and Joseph, but Aidan immediately said "Emma's parents". I could've kissed him.

Emma & Aidan